The Politics of NHS Reform 1988–97

Metaphor or reality?

The Politics of NHS Reform 1988–97

Metaphor or reality?

Chris Ham

Published by
King's Fund Publishing
11–13 Cavendish Square
London W1M 0AN

© King's Fund 2000

First published 2000

ISBN 1 85717 417 8

A CIP catalogue record for this book is available from the British Library

Available from:

King's Fund Bookshop
11–13 Cavendish Square
London
W1M 0AN

Tel: 020 7307 2591
Fax: 020 7307 2801

Printed and bound in Great Britain

Typeset by Peter Powell Origination & Print Limited

Photographs copyright PA Picture Library/Adam Butler/Jean Dempsey/
Jeff Gilbert/Tony Harris/David Jones/King's Fund/Stefan Rousseau

Contents

I recall my classes at Harvard. Some of my students used to regard public policy-making as a matter of finding the 'right' answer to a public problem. Politics was a set of obstacles which had to be circumvented so the 'right' answer could be implemented. Policy was clean – it could be done on computer. Politics was dirty – unpredictable, passionate, sometimes mean-spirited or corrupt. Policy was good; politics, a necessary evil.

I'd spend entire courses trying to disabuse them. I'd ask them how they knew they had the 'right' answer. They'd dazzle me with techniques – cost-benefit analyses, probability and statistics, regression analysis. Their mathematics was flawless. But – I'd ask it again – how did they know they had the right answer?

They never did. At most, policy wonks can help the public deliberate the likely consequences of various choices. But they can't presume to make the choices. Democracy is disorderly and sometimes dismaying, but it is the only source of wisdom on this score.

Next to the policy wonk who presumes to know what is best for the public sits the pollster who presumes to be able to tell what the public wants. The pollsters' techniques are just as flawed, and his conceit is no less dangerous to democracy. The public doesn't know what it wants until it has an opportunity to debate and consider. Engaging in a democratic process is not like choosing a favourite flavour of ice cream.

Politicians must lead; they must try to educate and persuade. They must enter into an ongoing dialogue with the public. No one can discover the 'best' policy through analytic prowess; nor is the 'best' policy that which happens to be the most popular on a questionnaire. Democracy requires deliberation and discussion. It entails public inquiry and discovery. Citizens need to be actively engaged. Political leaders must offer visions of the future and arguments to support the visions, and then must listen carefully for the response. A health-care plan devised by Plato's philosopher-king won't wash.

Reich, 1998, pp.107–08

Dedication

To the non-academic staff of the Health Services Management Centre, particularly Anne van der Salm and Sue Alleyne, whose hard work and excellence have contributed so much to the success of the Centre in the last decade.

Acknowledgements

I would like to thank the King's Fund for providing a grant to enable me to undertake the work reported here, and to Susan Elizabeth, the Fund's Grants Director, for her advice and comments as the work progressed. Thanks are also due to Virginia Bottomley, Kenneth Clarke, Stephen Dorrell and William Waldegrave for agreeing to be interviewed. At the University of Birmingham, David Marsh helped me relate my findings to the political science literature, and my assistant, Anne van der Salm, organised the fieldwork, transcribed the interviews, and helped turn my drafts into the final product. Nicholas Timmins and Andy McKeon read earlier drafts and offered valuable comments. I alone am responsible for what follows.

Chris Ham
October 1999

Foreword

Over the past decade or so, health policy has undergone major changes of direction. First the 'internal market', then the Patient's Charter, and now the *New NHS* and *Our Healthier Nation*. Those policies have affected the way all of us live, bringing fundamental changes to a public service used by almost everyone in society.

Yet the way those changes take place remains a mystery to most people. Why did the Conservative Government choose the internal market as a solution to a mounting crisis of confidence in the NHS in 1988? Why did the Labour Government, which opposed those reforms so vehemently when in Opposition, later retain so many of them in its own change of direction in health policy after 1997? Who made the decisions, and why, and how, did they get implemented?

This volume opens up some of those decision-making processes through a discussion with the four secretaries of state responsible for health between 1988 and 1997. It illustrates the tangled processes of challenging, bargaining and negotiating that shape the development of health policy in the political arena, from visions and ideas to plans and actions.

What comes out most clearly of all is the absence of the general public throughout the processes, except as voters whose confidence must be gained at election times. It is politicians, thinkers, interest groups and civil servants who are involved in a process of questioning or defending the status quo, building or opposing changes to established ways of working, without referring back to the public whose service the NHS is.

Health policy is about the wellbeing of the people. If those people are excluded from the processes of framing it, its effectiveness is almost certainly weakened. It is time for health policy to emerge from the shadows and become truly democratic.

Rabbi Julia Neuberger
Chief Executive of the King's Fund

Introduction

This book summarises the results of interviews with the four politicians who served as secretary of state for health between 1988 and 1997. The interviews were conducted during the second half of 1998, with the aim of capturing the views of the politicians concerned at a time when the events under discussion were still of relatively recent origin. The interview schedule was semi-structured and was intended primarily to encourage the interviewees to reflect on their experience in relation to the origins and implementation of the NHS reforms and other key health policy issues that arose during their time in office. A secondary purpose was to explore the 'world' in which health secretaries worked. This was done by asking questions about the sources of advice and support that were available, the organisations and people they saw as significant, and the way in which health secretaries were able to create time to think about the issues with which they were confronted.

The idea for the study reported here emerged out of my work in the politics of health care and the management of the NHS. In this work, I have been intrigued by the process by which policy ideas develop and are implemented and the part played in that process by politicians. Having had the opportunity to meet with health secretaries from time to time, and to observe them in action, I became increasingly interested in understanding their perspective on an important period in the evolution of the NHS. I was also fascinated by the pressures under which they operated, as empirical observation suggested that they were confronted with a challenging set of responsibilities that left little time for reflection. In these circumstances, where did politicians look to for advice, and who was most influential in the world in which they worked?

These are of course not new questions and there is a huge literature on the politics of health care and the management of the NHS. My previous writings in this area have focused mainly on the health policy-making process and have drawn on a range of concepts and theories, particularly from political science, to analyse the dynamics of the health policy community (Ham, 1999). This study adds to that literature by examining what light the testimony of politicians themselves sheds on the darker corners of policy-making. In so doing, it endeavours to tell the story of the NHS between 1988 and 1997 in the words of health secretaries themselves, recognising that while their perspective is only one among many it nevertheless offers an important viewpoint on events during that period.

In making connections between the recollections of health secretaries and the literature in this field, use is made where appropriate of the accounts of other significant players. However, the intention is not to provide a comprehensive analysis of the genesis and implementation of the NHS reforms, as this is beyond the scope of the present study. The objective of this book is altogether more modest: to explain how health secretaries saw developments and to relate their accounts to concepts and theories developed by political scientists who have studied health policy. Put another way, the findings are used to analyse the distribution of power within government, the relationship between government and outside interests, and the way in which policy agendas are set.

The chapters that follow can therefore be read at two levels. First, they present the narratives of politicians themselves on events during the period 1988–97. Second, these narratives contain clues about the policy-making process and the role of different actors in that process. To run ahead in the story, by talking to former health secretaries about their time in office, it is possible to address a range of themes in the academic literature on health policy and British government. These themes are reflected in the first three chapters and are drawn together for more detailed analysis in Chapter 4.

The book has been written with a variety of readers in mind. To begin with, it is aimed at those involved in health policy-making and implementation, whether in government or the NHS. It is also intended for teachers and students of health policy. The way in which the research reported here illustrates theoretical debates about policy networks, the role of pressure groups, and the influence of ministers and civil servants may make it of interest too to students of British government. Although not intended to be a guide for politicians, the book nevertheless offers warnings and lessons for those who may in future find themselves occupying the secretary of state's office in Richmond House.

The book is organised into four chapters. Chapter 1, Chronology, presents the evolution of policy between 1988 and 1997, from the perspective of the interviewees. Chapter 2, Policy, is organised on a thematic basis and discusses particular issues that were important during this period. Chapter 3, People, focuses on the individuals and organisations that populated the world of the health secretaries, and how they were perceived. Chapter 4, Analysis, reviews the material presented here for the lessons it holds for students of health policy-making.

Chapter 1

Chronology

In this chapter we summarise on a chronological basis the evidence gathered in the interviews. Developments between 1988 and 1997 are described using the Ministerial Review of the NHS as the starting point but picking up other key policy initiatives along the way. Figure 1 illustrates significant events during this period and provides the backcloth for the discussion.

Figure 1: The development of the NHS reforms

1988

January	Margaret Thatcher announces Ministerial Review of the NHS.
July	Department of Health created following the splitting-up of the Department of Health and Social Security.
	Kenneth Clarke appointed as Secretary of State for Health.

1989

January	*Working for Patients* published.
November	NHS and Community Care Bill published.

1990

June	NHS and Community Care Bill receives Royal Assent.
November	William Waldegrave replaces Kenneth Clarke as Secretary of State for Health.

1991

April	NHS reforms come into operation. The first wave of 57 NHS trusts and 306 GP fundholders is established in England.
October	The Patient's Charter published.

1992

April	The Conservative Party is re-elected. Virginia Bottomley replaces William Waldegrave as Secretary of State for Health. The second wave of 99 NHS trusts and 288 GP fundholders is established in England.
June	The King's Fund report on London's health services, *London Healthcare 2010*, is published.
July	A White Paper on *The Health of the Nation* is published.
October	The report of the Tomlinson Inquiry on London is published.

1993

February	The Government publishes its response to the Tomlinson Inquiry, *Making London Better*.

April	The third wave of 136 NHS trusts and over 600 GP fundholders is established in England.
October	The Government publishes its response to the functions and manpower review, *Managing the New NHS*. This includes the proposed abolition of regional health authorities, the merger of district health authorities and family health services authorities, and a streamlining of the NHS Management Executive.

1994

April	The fourth wave of 140 NHS trusts and 800 GP fundholders is established in England. The NHS Management Executive is renamed the NHS Executive and establishes eight regional offices. The number of regional health authorities is reduced from 14 to eight.
June	NHS performance tables published for the first time.
July	Department of Health publishes three reports, setting out plans to streamline the role of the Department and the NHS Executive.
December	*The Operation of the Internal Market: local freedoms, national responsibilities* published.

1995

January	An updated Patient's Charter published.
April	The fifth wave of 21 NHS trusts and 560 GP fundholders is established in England. An accountability framework for fundholders is introduced.
June	Health Authorities Bill receives Royal Assent.
July	Stephen Dorrell replaces Virginia Bottomley as Secretary of State for Health.
November	Plans to use the private finance initiative to build new NHS hospitals announced.

1996

April	Regional health authorities are abolished and their functions taken over by NHS Executive regional offices. District health authorities and family health services authorities replaced by unitary health authorities. The sixth wave of 1200 GP fundholders is established in England. Around 50 total purchasing projects go live.
May	Efficiency scrutiny into burdens of paperwork published.
June	Consultation paper *Primary Care: the future* published.
October	A White Paper on primary care, *Choice and Opportunity*, published. Reports of NHS funding problems.
November	A White Paper on the future of the NHS, *The National Health Service: A Service with Ambitions* published.
December	A second White Paper on primary care, *Primary care: delivering the future* published.

1997

March	NHS (Primary Care) Bill receives Royal Assent.
May	General election, in which Labour gains majority and forms a new Government.

Source: Adapted from Ham, 1997.

1988–90

Kenneth Clarke arrived at the Department of Health in July 1988. He took over this responsibility mid-way through the Ministerial Review of the NHS established by Margaret Thatcher in January 1988. Clarke's predecessor, John Moore, had presided over the Department of Health and Social Security but had become ill during the Review. The Prime Minister decided to divide the work of the Department, with Moore heading the Department of Social Security and Clarke taking over at the Department of Health. Clarke had served as a Minister of State for Health between 1982 and 1985 and this experience was to prove important in shaping the outcome of the Review.

Clarke described how the Review had originated:

> The NHS Review had been announced in a hurry the previous winter in the middle of what was becoming the annual financial crisis of the National Health Service ... The version I heard was that Margaret Thatcher had very unwisely accepted an invitation to go on the Panorama programme to sort out this NHS row. I think she probably intended to repeat all the statistics which she had been using ineffectively in the House of Commons for most of the winter to answer the row. At the last moment obviously she realised or was persuaded that this might not be sufficient. Therefore Bernard Ingham suggested to her that she should announce a review of the whole system and she went on and announced a review.

Clarke emphasised that 'The Review had remarkably little content at the time it was announced', adding that on his appointment as Secretary of State for Health he found that very little progress had been made. The lack of progress was, he felt, one of the reasons for his appointment. The Prime Minister had given a commitment to complete the Review within a year and there was a need to bring the thinking together to enable the Government to present its proposals for reform. Clarke's previous experience as a Minister of State for Health was important because it meant that the Prime Minister:

> ... was able to appoint somebody to the National Health Service who had no particular learning curve to go through and who would therefore be able to pick it up quickly and who could start work straight away as it were. If somebody totally new to the health service had been brought in common sense, I think, would have dictated that about six months would have to elapse before the new incumbent felt 'at home' with this rather peculiar institution.

He added that he had not expected to return to the Health Department because his views on the NHS did not coincide with the Prime Minister's. This difference of approach was confirmed when John Moore briefed Clarke on the work that had been done in the first half of 1988. Clarke recalled that:

> My conversation with him wasn't very reassuring. It became obvious that John was sold, as I knew Margaret Thatcher was, on the idea that really we should go into a system of compulsory private insurance. John was particularly pleased to tell me that he had already got Margaret to agree on large extensions of tax relief for employers and for individuals engaged in private insurance and that the Treasury were proving awkward, but with Margaret's help I should be able to overcome Treasury resistance. I don't remember responding very actively to this news because personally I thought that approach to reforming the National Health Service was completely hopeless. I was personally opposed to it and I thought it was bad tax policy to start giving tax reliefs of this kind. More importantly, I thought insurance-based systems were not the answer and have not been a great success, either in the United States, or in the United Kingdom in the private sector. They are just very high cost with insurance companies as a useless intermediary. And I didn't think this was an adequate review at all. My views were much more managerial.

It was because of his reservations about moving away from tax funding of the NHS that Clarke focused more on the *delivery* of health services than their financing. Some work on options for strengthening the management of the NHS had been started before his appointment but it was given additional impetus by the change of secretary of state. In the second half of the Review, attention focused almost entirely on NHS management. Clarke explained that his previous experience in the health portfolio, which included overseeing the introduction of the Griffiths general management reforms, had been important in shaping his own thinking:

> … my views had been formed at the time when I was Minister of State, where there was nothing fundamentally wrong with the National Health Service's basic premise that you provided treatment free at the time of delivery to everybody, strove to deliver the highest quality health care by global standards and that you paid for it out of general taxation. What I thought was that turning that into practice was a very superhuman challenge and that the management structures, the awful bureaucracy, were inadequate to deliver that.

Kenneth Clarke MP, Health Secretary, 1988–90.

It followed from this diagnosis that changing the structure of the NHS and reducing bureaucracy had, in Clarke's view, to be central to any attempt to reform the NHS. His opinion was that:

> ... *if you were going for managerial reforms, I was an adherent, and still am actually, to what was the then increasingly fashionable view of how you managed large organisations, which is to delegate responsibility downwards and to make people accountable upwards.*

Clarke had inherited some thinking on management reform in respect of hospitals. Stimulated by the views of doctors and others, the idea of self-governing NHS hospitals had emerged, and he explained:

> *It was new to me and I spent some time exploring that ... Eventually, after I had, amongst other things, debated how to find a more user-friendly title than 'self-governing hospital', which I tended to use at first, that became the idea of the NHS trust.*

Clarke's personal contribution to the Review was more apparent in the idea of general practitioner fundholding. On being appointed and reading the papers that had been written up to that point, he was struck by the absence of references to general practitioners, particularly as his view was that:

> ... *the whole key to the British system of health care was that we had this family doctor system, which I continue to believe is its principal strength vis-à-vis other health care systems in the world.*

The proposal to give GPs budgets with which to buy some services for patients was intended to strengthen the UK family doctor system and to reinforce the role of the GP as the agent of patients. While the idea had been discussed in academic literature and had been advocated by various contributors to the Review, Clarke recalled:

> ... *as far as I personally was concerned, I devised this on my holiday in Galicia when the press back home were hunting for me as the missing minister on a completely spurious newspaper story that I should come back to take part in some talks on nurse grading which actually couldn't take place because not only was I abroad on holiday but so were all the trade union leaders.*

By the autumn of 1988 NHS trusts and GP fundholding had therefore become the main building blocks of the Government's plans to strengthen the management of the NHS and to create greater incentives for efficiency. The other key proposal was that responsibility for purchasing care and providing services should be separated in order to create the conditions for an internal market. This proposal derived from the writings of an American economist, Alain Enthoven, who in 1985 had published his ideas for reforming the NHS (Enthoven, 1985). Clarke explained that when Enthoven's ideas had first appeared he had not been convinced of their merits:

> *Enthoven had set this whole debate running just as I was leaving from being Minister of State … And my first reaction was sceptical. I was still immersed in what was then the Griffiths reforms. And I thought he was, well what shall I say, a right wing sort of eccentric who I don't agree with. It was when I came back, I think I kept Enthoven's article, and saw where they were, once I got over my initial surprise almost, and everything had moved on from then, but Enthoven's original idea was actually the germ of the idea.*

Fundholding had not featured in Enthoven's proposal, which identified health authorities as the purchasers in the internal market. Giving GPs control over budgets appealed to Clarke because of the need to ensure that purchasing decisions were sensitive to the needs of patients and also because patients themselves were not well placed to be purchasers. In his view it followed that:

> *… if you are going to be steered to the best place in the system you need an expert gatekeeper and guide and the GP, a good GP, is the best person to act on your behalf because he has your interests in mind, he knows you and your family and he is the person who should be able to discharge the task of steering you properly into the health care system. And I therefore thought that if you were talking about in whose hands we were going to place the money to enable more patient oriented judgements to be made on priorities, then the obvious answer was general practitioners … .*

Clarke's plans differed from Enthoven's in one other important respect. This was in his dislike of the phrase 'internal market', an aversion which (as we shall see) was shared by his successors. In place of 'internal market', Clarke preferred to describe the reforms as involving a 'purchaser/provider divide'. He explained:

> ... I used 'purchaser' to mean those who should be assessing patient-based priorities and deciding where to devote public resources to obtain those services, and I used the word 'provider' to mean those who managed the delivery of the services in response to whatever the 'purchasers' were stipulating as the public interest. That was my starting point. I tried to build in a concentration on quality as well as sheer quantity of service and some appraisal of results.

The final form of the Government's plans was hammered out in a series of discussions in the committee responsible for the Review, chaired by the Prime Minister. Clarke recalled of the committee:

> ... I think its only members were Margaret chairing it, me, Nigel Lawson, and occasionally the chief secretary, John Major, would come, but not to every meeting I don't think ... It had as a secretary Richard Wilson who's now the Cabinet secretary whose unenviable task it was to go away and write up the minutes of these meetings which were extremely enjoyable, furious and robust debate for most of the time.

Although the arguments in the committee were 'very robust', Clarke emphasised that:

> Richard Wilson was brilliant at sorting out minutes that were usable to people who had to read the minutes and decide what to do next. My private office told me that they always used to ring up before I got back to the Department to see what mood I'd be in when I got back, and Richard used to cheer me up after the debates thrashing out the reforms and say, 'if you think these are lively meetings you should have been with Kenneth Baker in Education'. He thought we weren't in the same league of disputes with Margaret as Ken Baker. But that's Margaret's working style. It was my working style. It was Nigel Lawson's working style. We didn't fall out personally but we got very, very worked up with each other. That was how she thrashed out decisions ... It was a Government that ran on willpower.

At the heart of this debate was the issue that had dominated the early stages of the Review – tax relief on private medical insurance. This had been advocated not only by John Moore but also by the Prime Minister, Clarke explaining:

Margaret thought that anybody who could afford to should pay for their own health. She thought it was not a function of the state. She could never understand why people, Willie Whitelaw as well as I, used to be rather proud of the fact that we used the National Health Service. She thought we should be ashamed that people like ourselves who could afford to pay for ourselves required the taxpayer to pay such a basic expense for our family. She therefore wanted to put far more people standing on their own feet and encourage people to spend their money on something sensible like health by giving them tax relief. A perfectly reputable view, just happened to be not one I shared ... .

The use of tax relief was opposed by the Chancellor of the Exchequer, Nigel Lawson, as well as by Clarke, and both agreed to give way to the Prime Minister only on the question of tax relief for elderly people – in Clarke's words, 'this last vestigial remains of Margaret's original idea'. Clarke's opposition to private medical insurance and his conviction that the basic principles of the NHS were fundamentally sound led Virginia Bottomley to comment that 'Ken Clarke deserves the credit for saving the NHS', adding that 'It was ironic that he got so castigated by the doctors'.

Another issue that provoked debate at this stage in the Review was fundholding. In this case, there was disagreement between the Treasury and the Department of Health. Debate centred on the Treasury's concerns about the loss of control that might result from the introduction of fundholding. As Clarke recalled:

it was counter cultural to the Treasury public spending function that the Government should be handing over control of huge, vast sums of money, to all these people all over the country who wanted to spend it.

In making this observation, Clarke drew a distinction between the Treasury as an institution and the ministers at its head. At the time these ministers included John Major as well as Nigel Lawson and both were open to persuasion on the question of fundholding:

Nigel used to stick to the brief occasionally but being Nigel would eventually come off it, and Nigel's a brilliantly intelligent man, and he's able to think on his feet, think on his bottom at a meeting, and will be constructive, just a valuable chap to have in any discussion. So Nigel was perfectly amenable to argument as long as you were capable of arguing in these ferocious debates and

*of course he'd agree with me on some things and not with Margaret. John
Major was quite helpful because at that time he had huge influence on
Margaret. John rather shared my rather more pro-NHS views and I think
John Major was much more attracted by the patient orientation that we kept
trying to give it. John was very, very useful.*

The White Paper that set out the Government's proposals was published in
January 1989. *Working for Patients* provoked a storm of protest and opposition
from the medical profession (Secretary of State for Health and others, 1989).
This did not surprise Clarke, whose experience as Minister of State for Health
had alerted him to the strength of the BMA and the royal medical colleges.
He explained that:

*I came from my experience as Minister of State feeling it was bound to be a
battleground. One of my repeated phrases when I was there was 'we are
picking up every tablet of stone in Tavistock House and we are smashing it on
the pavement in front of the building, the BMA will fight this and they will
fight to win'. They are the most unscrupulous trade union I have ever dealt
with and I've dealt with every trade union across the board. My opinion was
you get your retaliation in first as this is going to be war.*

Relationships with the BMA were complicated by the negotiations taking
place at the same time on a new contract for GPs. Clarke described how these
negotiations had begun when he had been Minister of State and were
unresolved on his return to the Department as Secretary of State. He confessed
that he was 'horrified' to find that this was the case, and 'I drove it through and
really bullied the negotiators into a settlement'. Part of the problem was that
the doctors' negotiators couldn't guarantee to deliver their members and
'It was just war all the way'.

Clarke recognised that his belligerent stance on the GPs' contract contributed
to the conflict with the BMA on the NHS reforms, arguing that 'The downside
at the time of the reforms was obviously the appalling relations with everybody
in the Service'. This led to difficulties within the Department of Health, with
'The bulk of the Department ... resistant to the whole idea' because 'The
tradition of the Department was based on allowing all these interest groups just
to run the whole damn thing'. Even more importantly, the Prime Minister
became concerned at the potential consequences of continuing opposition
from the BMA with a general election approaching. With all the preparations
in place to launch the reforms in April 1991, Clarke recalled that:

*at the very last moment … somebody persuaded Margaret that this would be a
disaster, that this would destroy her Government … Charlie Haughey, who I
don't think Margaret had an unstinting regard for, had persuaded her that the
key to elections in Ireland he was sure was never to fight with the doctors. She
got this into her head. She then suddenly decided that it would have to be
postponed until after the next election.*

To confirm this view, the Prime Minister asked a group of businessmen to make
an assessment of whether the NHS reforms would work. Clarke explained that:

*they universally came back and said 'no they wouldn't, it needed years more
work'. They said the ideas were good. They were supportive of the reforms.
But their advice, because we had no means of costing anything we were doing,
which was certainly true, was that we must delay implementation. My idea
always was that it would evolve. Get it in and then let it evolve. But they
advised that there was so little financial information, again true, the NHS was
so unbelievably bereft of accurate management information, that nobody
could manage the system.*

The upshot was a meeting at 10 Downing Street in June 1990 between the
Prime Minister and the businessmen who had advised her, and the Secretary of
State and his officials. Among the latter group, the key members were Duncan
Nichol, chief executive of the NHS, Peter Griffiths, his deputy, and Sheila
Masters, director of finance. Clarke had a high opinion of these officials and a
younger group of civil servants whom he took along to the meeting. In his words:

*They were a brilliant outfit so I left them to present themselves. I said that the
team would do a presentation, they will explain to you. She wanted to see who
was going to run this … Normally, they would have done themselves justice,
they would have outshone the outsiders, they just knew more about it.*

In fact, it did not turn out like that and 'they all let themselves down'. Clarke
recalled how, observing:

*I sat there curled up really. The reason was, not that they all had a party the
night before or anything, but what I hadn't appreciated was that they were of
course terribly overawed. They were in the Cabinet Room at No.10, they
were facing the Prime Minister. I'd worked for Margaret for ten years so I was
used to her style, her interrupting, but to my team this was like going to see the*

Queen in an earlier era. They were quite obviously curled up and every time she interrupted she got blushes and stammers in reply ... Then the businessmen rather sheepishly came out with their rehearsed views. They weren't much good either and it wound up with another debate between Margaret and myself.

The outcome of this debate was that Clarke eventually got his way. He persuaded the Prime Minister that postponing implementation of the reforms was not a sensible option and she grudgingly allowed him to proceed. One of the considerations in Clarke's thinking was that it was better to proceed and to demonstrate that the worst fears of the Government's critics were not realised than to delay and to allow the Opposition to capitalise on the concerns expressed by the medical profession. Clarke's determination to see the reforms through was also a factor and he recalled:

the reason I was able to talk her out of it was she did realise she couldn't possibly cancel it faced with a Secretary of State who'd spent two years on it, who was as committed to it as I was, so worked up about the idea of postponing it. The whole meeting had been intended to persuade me that all we were doing was postponing it until after the election but it became, as a result of one of our usual cheery exchanges, quite obvious that she wasn't going to persuade me.

The Prime Minister did not forget this dispute and at the first opportunity she moved Clarke on to Education. Clarke would have preferred to stay on to launch the reforms and he remembered:

Trying to avoid being reshuffled, I had said to Margaret 'I know it's a bit like a rocket that was all steaming away on the pad and all you had to do was press the button'. For all I knew it might blow up 100 yards in the air, but my judgement was that it was going to work.

Clarke's wish to see the job through was not granted, and he explained:

What she then did, when she got an opportunity she didn't want, which was when Geoffrey Howe resigned, was move me away from Health to Education where she wanted education reforms livened up and put into Health William [Waldegrave], giving William a clear remit to calm it all down and be nice to the doctors.

1990–92

William Waldegrave confirmed that this was indeed the remit he had been given by the Prime Minister on his appointment in November 1990. He came to the Department of Health as reluctantly as Clarke left, having been closely involved in preparations for the Gulf War in his previous post at the Foreign Office. Waldegrave felt his skills fitted him better for that role than for the Health brief, which he described as 'completely new territory to me'. He was also aware that 'succeeding Kenneth would not be an easy task because I greatly admired Ken and knew that he didn't want to be moved at that moment'. Waldegrave felt that his background in industry suited him more to a department like Transport or Energy than Health and it was therefore with some trepidation that he accepted his new brief.

Waldegrave remembered the Prime Minister saying to him 'Kenneth has stirred them all up now you have to calm them down'. The first big decision he was faced with was the one that Clarke thought he had resolved and won, namely whether to proceed with the reforms or whether to postpone their implementation. Waldegrave described how:

> *huge pressure came to bear straight away from all the obvious suspects such as the BMA but also from backbenchers and to some extent from No.10 … to say, 'do we have to go on with all this reform, can't we delay, can't we go slower?'*

Margaret Thatcher was not personally involved in this process because immediately after Waldegrave's appointment she was thrown into the crisis of her own leadership of the Conservative Party, which led to her replacement by John Major. Nevertheless, Waldegrave emphasised that if he had chosen to he could have postponed the introduction of the reforms even at that late stage. He decided not to and described this decision as 'in a way, the most important single thing I did as Secretary of State'. The reason for this was that:

> *having been launched down this path with a coherent rational scheme of reform to which the best people, I thought, within the management were deeply committed, to have backed off at that point would have been chaos. And of course the BMA wouldn't have stopped lobbying. They'd have just moved the boundaries and started lobbying against whatever else one was doing. So I am sure that was the right decision. But it then meant a huge rush of going up a learning curve for me and in a sense it meant that from that moment I was committed to supporting Duncan [Nichol], which I don't regret at all.*

Waldegrave's support for the reforms was reinforced by the backing they received from politicians like David Owen as well as from academics such as Alain Enthoven. As he explained:

> it personally attracted me that this was a radical centrist policy. My ... own instincts in politics are not unradical but are centrist. I don't think there is any contradiction between the two. So I liked the idea that there was [an] Enthoven-Owen-Clarke body of opinion behind all that.

Having taken the decision to proceed, the next major issue Waldegrave had to confront was how many NHS trusts to establish in the first wave, which was to come into operation in April 1991. On this issue there were differences of opinion within the Department of Health, particularly between Duncan Nichol and Sheila Masters. The Department had received 178 expressions of interest from the providers of hospital and community health services to become NHS trusts in June 1989 and this was reduced to 79 applications by the end of that year. In considering these applications, Waldegrave explained that the Government needed to establish a reasonable number of trusts to avoid the reforms being seen as 'a damp squib'. The key judgement was what number was reasonable given the concern to avoid supporting applications from providers who saw trust status as a route to survival or from those that were not viable financially. As director of finance, Sheila Masters was more cautious than Duncan Nichol who, in Waldegrave's words, 'was on the side all the time saying, "well let them try, they want to, why shouldn't they be allowed to try?"', whereas 'Sheila was saying, "where are the reserves? Look at this, it's not viable, where's the income?"'. In the event 57 NHS trusts were launched in April 1991, Waldegrave reporting that in retrospect he felt an appropriate balance had been struck between supporting the enthusiasts and not going ahead with those that were financial risks.

The prudence displayed in relation to NHS trusts was also apparent in the message that went out to staff in the NHS that the new Secretary of State wanted to achieve a 'smooth take off' for the reforms. Waldegrave reported that on this issue there was a consensus within the Department of Health. Part of the rationale of a smooth take off was political, with the impending general election casting a long shadow forward and leading to the development of guidance designed to ensure a 'steady state' in the first year of contracting between purchasers and providers. Equally important in Waldegrave's view was the influence of private sector experience brought by himself and officials like Sheila Masters, who had been seconded from KPMG.

William Waldegrave MP, Health Secretary, 1990–92.

This experience cautioned against rapid or sudden changes in where services were provided. As Waldegrave reflected:

> I had had enough private sector experience myself in GEC to know this, that there were some pretty naïve ideas about how competitive purchasing worked. I mean good firms don't change their suppliers every three minutes just to keep them on their toes. You try and develop good supportive relationships with your key suppliers. You go right down the production chain if you are a sensible firm. When I was buying steel for GEC one used to spend a lot of time talking to the steel makers in Sheffield ... about what was going on and what their work practices were and were they reliable and was there anything we could do to help. If they get wildly out of line then you have to change them but you try and have a co-operative relationship. So I hope that, again supported by Sheila in that, I tried to stop some of the more gung-ho people thinking that it was all 'we are the masters now, we can fire all these miserable surgeons who haven't been doing what we want'.

Experience of implementing the reforms had the effect of persuading Waldegrave of the merits of fundholding. He recalled that 'Kenneth had certainly been very personally attached to the idea of GP fundholders and that was always the area where I was least clear, at the beginning at any rate'. What changed Waldegrave's mind was seeing what fundholders had achieved. He described how:

> I did come to the conclusion that there was the unleashing here of a potential for very great improvement, partly because of what I saw when I actually went and talked to GPs in their own surgeries and so on. It was rather like talking to headmistresses and headmasters in schools at the time when we were beginning to launch local budgets for schools. One really could see the savings that they could make and so on. So I became increasingly convinced by GP fundholding and committed to it.

Waldegrave's thinking on the reforms as a whole was strongly influenced by his view that the application of market principles to health care was highly constrained. This meant that, like Kenneth Clarke before him, he was hesitant about using the vocabulary of competition. As he explained:

> the language of dynamic benchmarking is really better than that of the market. The power of the system was the capacity to compare outcomes and cost all the time against a big enough system so that it was innovating all the time and it was generating new and better practices all the time.

The change of language served another purpose by helping to reassure the health professions about the Government's intentions and reinforcing the calming effect desired by Margaret Thatcher when she appointed Waldegrave. Despite this, there continued to be concerns about the impact of the reforms and these concerns were felt most strongly in London. The Government was forced to set up an independent inquiry under Professor Bernard Tomlinson to make proposals for rationalising the provision of services in the capital. Waldegrave explained how he was 'naïve about London' in that he felt aligning services more closely with the population and its needs was necessary and 'I thought that anybody could see the logic of it'. What he had not bargained for was the power of the press in London and the strength of public and professional opposition to changes in well-established hospital services. Reflecting on this he felt that:

> in retrospect … I think there was more that could have been done to have prepared for a better outcome in London and perhaps the answer is … you just have to have a strong government that has the courage to do it.

Waldegrave's main personal contribution to the development of policy during this period was to give priority to the Green Paper setting out the national health strategy, *The Health of the Nation* (Secretary of State for Health, 1991). This was not unrelated to his aim of overcoming the opposition of doctors and nurses to the Government's plans in that, by focusing on the issue of health and outcomes, *The Health of the Nation* opened up an agenda that spoke more directly to the concerns of many NHS staff than the changes that followed from *Working for Patients*. Waldegrave emphasised that publishing the health strategy did not happen without a struggle. In particular, Kenneth Clarke was opposed to the Government telling people what to do, and he was against the setting of targets for improving the health of the population, which the Government could do little to influence. Waldegrave recalled how Clarke:

> led the opposition in various Cabinet committees to the Green Paper and constant sniping went on in Cabinet debate, and he was then easily able to stir up the right wing, he was rather cynical about this, but I think he believed it.

Waldegrave also presided over the publication of the Patient's Charter. This stemmed from the initiative taken by John Major across government as a whole to develop explicit standards of service delivery from the perspective of citizens and service users. Waldegrave was a strong supporter of the Patient's Charter:

because again it moved the conversation to outcomes. And it fitted actually frightfully well with the internal market reforms because the whole purpose of the benchmarking if you like was to be able to compare the quality of what was on offer.

His only regret in relation to the Patient's Charter was not to push harder for the development of measures of clinical outcome and the publication of the results. Against this, Waldegrave summarised his main achievements as:

Pushing on with the reforms. Not letting it fall to pieces, not giving in to the initial pressure. Launching The Health of the Nation *... and the Charter as trying to shift towards health status and outcomes.*

However, his time in office was not all plain sailing. In the early months of his tenure a series of newspaper reports raised questions about Waldegrave's position, requiring the Prime Minister to express his confidence in the Secretary of State. Criticism came from the right of the Conservative Party as well as the left, with Waldegrave's critics arguing that both he and John Major were betraying their Thatcherite inheritance. Unfavourable comparisons were also made with Kenneth Clarke, whose robust style was felt by some members of the Party to be more effective than Waldegrave's conciliatory approach. While Waldegrave rode out the storm with the support of the Prime Minister, the difficulties he encountered illustrated the fine line secretaries of state have to walk between confrontation and appeasement.

Throughout this period, the reforms to the NHS remained at the heart of the debate between the political parties, and health issues figured prominently both in by-elections and the 1992 general election. In October 1991, the chief executive of the NHS, Duncan Nichol, entered this debate by giving an interview to the *Daily Mail*, in which he denied the Government's plans were designed to privatise health services. Nichol's comments were criticised by the Opposition parties who argued that as a civil servant Nichol should have remained neutral on this issue. Waldegrave took the view that there was nothing wrong with the interview, adding 'I do not see how the chief manager of the Service could have said anything other than that he was committed to the reforms'. Waldegrave also felt that the Labour Party overplayed its hand on the NHS with exaggerated claims that the Government was going down the path of privatisation and the controversy that surrounded the party political broadcast on Jennifer's ear during the general election. In retrospect, the 1992 general election can be viewed as a watershed in that after the election the Labour Party adopted a more discriminating response to the reforms, abandoning its outright opposition and taking on board some of the changes that had been introduced when shaping its own approach.

1992–95

It fell to Waldegrave's Minister of State, Virginia Bottomley, to take over as Secretary of State after the election in April 1992. Bottomley had also served under Clarke and, as she commented:

> *I knew that it was a job where you had a honeymoon where you were praised and then it was really tough pounding and in the end like people shooting at targets at a fairground. They get you in the end. My pa used to say, 'nobody gets a salary and a round of applause'.*

Bottomley was here referring to the problems Waldegrave had encountered during the election campaign. As she commented, 'somehow it had gone wrong for William and the Jennifer's ear problems and so he was kept out of radio contact for much of the campaign'. She was also anticipating difficulties she was to confront after the honeymoon period had ended.

On appointment, Bottomley's main aim was 'to ensure that the reforms were so well established … that they would no longer be part of the party political debate'. In practice this meant 'I wanted to get trusts completed. I wanted to get beyond 50 per cent on GP fundholders … I wanted the Patient's Charter to continue to deliver'. The emphasis was on implementing the reforms step by step because:

> *we needed to make haste quietly – just keep on, keep our eye on the ball at completing the changes – assuming that the easiest trusts had gone ahead, that there would be all sorts of glitches. The idea is easy but the implementation and delivery is the crucial issue and I much appreciated having Duncan Nichol there.*

One of Bottomley's major challenges was London, which Waldegrave, in his own words, had 'played … past the election'. Because of her own association with hospitals like Bart's, Guy's and St Thomas's, the Secretary of State asked her Minister of State, Brian Mawhinney, to take a lead on individual cases while she maintained the momentum across London as a whole. She explained that 'my contribution was to say, "people should really go through this

Virginia Bottomley MP, Health Secretary, 1992–95.

together". It was vital that we should try and get decisions through, bring uncertainty to an end'. Just as Margaret Thatcher had pushed through her economic policies with determination in the 1980s, so Bottomley felt that she had the task of making the right decisions for London – even at the risk of personal unpopularity. She recognised that John Major might have been drawn in to the process but she turned down his offers of help, preferring instead to carry the responsibility. Doing so was difficult but Bottomley insisted on staying on to see the job through despite being offered other Cabinet posts. Although not all her objectives were achieved, either in relation to London or other issues, by the time she moved on in July 1995 she felt that 'I'd done what I needed to do,' and 'the overall forward march was quite positive'.

Doing what she needed to do included not only continuing with the initiatives launched by her predecessors but also making her own mark on the policy agenda. This included putting in place the research and development programme, including the commitment to promote evidence-based medicine, streamlining the organisation of the NHS through the decision to merge district health authorities and family health services authorities and to abolish regional health authorities, and continuing with the implementation of the community care reforms. Bottomley also took action to reduce waiting times for treatment in line with the commitment contained in the Patient's Charter, and she initiated measures to cut the hours worked by junior doctors. One of her particular interests was women's issues, including giving priority to the adoption of 'women-friendly employment practices' in the NHS and to Opportunity 2000, a programme designed to increase the participation of women in the workforce at all levels.

Towards the end of her time in this post, Bottomley gave a number of speeches in which she reflected on what had been achieved and the direction the reforms were taking. Most notably, in a lecture at the Royal Society of Medicine in June 1995, she reiterated the Government's commitment to the principles of the NHS and argued that the policy framework represented by the Patient's Charter, *The Health of the Nation*, and the research and development strategy was a coherent programme of policies. Bottomley went on to emphasise that the central bureaucratic structures of the NHS had been replaced by greater local responsibility for decision-making and increased diversity and innovation. Notwithstanding this, there remained a need for strategic oversight:

A great deal can and will be achieved through the purchaser/provider system. As that relationship matures, I want to see purchasing become more sophisticated. I want to see greater use of longer-term contracts between health authorities, fundholders and NHS trusts.

We need more imagination in contracting so that it doesn't simply replicate the habits of the past but reaches out to the future. Decisions should be motivated not just by cost but by long-term improvements in quality and outcomes, in health and in meeting a range of needs in different settings.

The new NHS requires a strategic oversight … The implementation of our strategy for developing cancer services is just one example of where we shall achieve a long-term goal by working together within the framework offered by the new NHS.

(Bottomley, 1995)

The significance of this statement, and indeed of the speech as a whole, was in providing a rationale and restatement of the purpose of the reforms four years into their implementation.

1995–97

Bottomley's successor, Stephen Dorrell, also came to the post with previous experience as a junior minister in the Department in the early 1990s. Like Clarke and Bottomley, he was therefore able to 'hit the ground running'. He described his inheritance as one in which:

Virginia, in her first couple of years, had been basically well received and been regarded, at least in the political community, as having been a success as Health Secretary, and I think in her last year in the Department, perhaps inevitably, it's probably a story of many previous health secretaries as well, she'd got into rather deeper water, pre-eminently as far as the political community was concerned, around the London reorganisation.

Dorrell was at pains to point out early on during his term of office that:

I didn't envisage a sort of Maoist … continuing revolution in the health service, that I felt that the basic high octane, high drama, managerial reform process let's say had run its course, but the line – the rules of the game – were

by then pretty clear and what we'd done essentially was to put in place a
machinery which was intended to be a more effective means of keeping the
health service up to date, making it more flexible and responsive to changing
patient demands, changing medical practice, etc. And so I was accurately
reported in a Sunday newspaper as saying that the NHS reform process was
essentially yesterday's story and what we were now committed to was trying to
make the new structure work effectively to the benefit of patients.

Commentaries on Dorrell's appointment emphasised the contrast between his
style and that of Virginia Bottomley, the new Secretary of State being seen as
more willing to listen and to explain the Government's policies and less
concerned to defend the reforms at every opportunity.

In relation to London, Dorrell recalled the Prime Minister telling him on his
appointment that 'Virginia had made a series of very difficult and tough
decisions in London and I was fortunate that they had been made'. Dorrell
himself emphasised that he had no intention of reopening issues that had
already been resolved. Instead, he turned his attention to two immediate
problems that needed to be tackled, namely a dispute with nurses over the
introduction of flexible local pay arrangements and the future of out-of-hours
provision by GPs. Both issues were settled quite quickly, with the out-of-hours
debate leading into a review of policy in the primary care field culminating in
the publication of two White Papers and the NHS (Primary Care) Act 1997.

Looking beyond primary care, Dorrell started work on a White Paper on the
future of the NHS, building on speeches that Bottomley had given during the
final period of her tenure as Secretary of State, and in the process seeking to
draw a line in the sand in relation to the acrimonious debates that had
characterised health policy in the early 1990s. Dorrell's efforts found
expression in *The NHS: A Service with Ambitions*, published in 1996 (Secretary
of State for Health, 1996). As he explained:

I wanted to try to convey the message we were interested in thinking forward
what the health service needed to look like and ... the challenges it needed to
look forward to face in the next Parliament and through into the next century,
etc. And that became more important to me as a political objective as the
Parliament drew to its close because otherwise it's the old business in politics
that, particularly when the opinion polls were running as they were, that trying
to persuade anybody that you were looking beyond the last likely date for
polling day is something of an uphill struggle, so conveying the impression that
this is a forward looking exercise was important. That's where it came from.

Stephen Dorrell MP, Health Secretary, 1995–97.

As the work on the White Paper proceeded, another objective that Dorrell saw as important was to stimulate thinking within the NHS on some of the key challenges for the future. These challenges included ensuring high standards of care, delivering a seamless service and workforce planning. He saw these as issues that were not controversial in party political terms but ones that needed to be addressed to sustain the NHS into the next century. Indeed, Dorrell went further to reiterate, like Bottomley, Waldegrave and Clarke before him, his personal commitment to the NHS and his aim in the White Paper of developing a programme of work that would strengthen the NHS model and not undermine it. The proposals in *The NHS: A Service with Ambitions* were entirely consistent with this approach, restating the Government's commitment to the founding principles of the NHS, and initiating a programme of work on information and IT, professional development and the quality of care.

In relation to the organisation of the NHS, Dorrell took over as Secretary of State at a time when decisions on the abolition of regional health authorities and the merger of district health authorities and family health services authorities had been taken. He saw his job as ensuring that they were implemented. The main decision he was confronted with was the number and configuration of NHS trusts. He recalled:

> When I got there, there was a beginnings of an argument that said that what we needed was a whole lot of trust reorganisations. And that I poured quite a lot of cold water on.

The reason for this was that the NHS had been through a series of management changes and Dorrell felt that a period of relative stability was needed to make the changes work. More important in his view was paying attention to service delivery issues like the pressure of emergency admissions to hospitals in the winter months. On this issue, he acted to ensure that the number of paediatric intensive care beds was increased to deal with rising demands, and he established a reporting system to monitor bed availability in different hospitals and to share the information more effectively.

To make this point is to illustrate how the terms of the health policy debate had shifted in the period since 1989. Whereas at the outset the preoccupation of ministers was with the introduction of a series of radical and controversial reforms to the NHS, by the time of the 1997 general election these reforms had not only been implemented in large part, they had also been assimilated and, to a considerable degree, accepted. In relation to the party political debate on the NHS, the differences between the Conservatives and Labour had narrowed as a result of movements on both sides. In part, this stemmed from the willingness of 'New Labour' under Tony Blair to use aspects of the Conservatives' reforms to pursue its own priorities for the NHS, and in part it resulted from changes made by Conservative Secretaries of State to both the substance of these reforms and their presentation. The latter was most evident in relation to the introduction of market principles and the way in which the emphasis on competition was replaced with a focus on the management aspects of the changes. We examine this shift in more detail in Chapter 2.

Summary: The development of policy, 1988–97

The evidence summarised here highlights the complexities involved in health policy-making between 1988 and 1997. Two points deserve emphasis. First, the Ministerial Review of the NHS was announced without warning and with no clear idea at the outset as to what would emerge. Far from representing an example of an ideologically inspired government seeking to impose its pre-ordained solutions on to the NHS, the Review created an opportunity for different interests to put forward their preferred ideas. The eventual outcome reflected the debate and discussion that took place between the Prime Minister, the Chancellor of the Exchequer and the Health Secretary. To be sure, the internal market bore all the hallmarks of Thatcherite thinking, but in its rejection of alternative sources of financing and other radical options it came as a disappointment to organisations and individuals on the centre-right of politics who had hoped for far-reaching solutions. The Prime Minister's instincts were thwarted by Treasury opposition to moving away from taxation as the main source of health service funding, and by Kenneth Clarke's commitment to the principles of the NHS and his preference for changes to management rather than funding. The detail of the package to emerge was shaped in discussion with civil servants and advisers, although organisations normally closely involved in policy development – like the BMA and NHS managers – were excluded from the process.

Second, the accounts of the health secretaries indicate that politicians were continuously making calculations about the effects of their policies and adjusting course in the process. Even Margaret Thatcher, widely seen at the time as a conviction politician par excellence, harboured some doubts about the changes she had set in train, and only acquiesced with reluctance to Kenneth Clarke's wish to move ahead with implementation. One of the consequences was that policy was modified during implementation in relation to its presentation, the pace of change and the substance of what was pursued. The potential for policy to be adapted during implementation was enhanced by the broad framework set out in *Working for Patients*, which omitted many of the details of how the internal market was intended to work and left scope for interpretation by those in the Department of Health and the NHS. It was as a result of this emergent strategy that the shape of the new NHS eventually became clear.

Chapter 2

Policy

In this chapter we analyse developments between 1988 and 1997 on a thematic basis. The chapter begins by reviewing how the concept and presentation of the internal market was modified over time and goes on to discuss the challenge presented by London, the development of the national health strategy, policy on primary care, public expenditure and private finance, and the relocation of the NHS Executive to Leeds.

Markets or management?

Kenneth Clarke's reluctance to use the phrase 'internal market' and his preference for 'purchaser/provider divide' set a precedent that other health secretaries were to follow. Clarke's views were based on the argument that the NHS reforms built on the Griffiths general management changes with which he had been closely involved in the early 1980s. As such, they were more concerned with the delegation of management responsibility than the introduction of competition. Clarke's position was reinforced by subsequent experiences in other government departments. As he recalled:

> I had been full-time in the health service for three-and-a-half years in the not too distant past when my agenda had been dominated by managerial change with the help of Roy Griffiths. So to my own satisfaction, if nobody else's, I hit the board running and had a pretty clear idea what I wished to do; and I had been in DTI, I had been in Employment, I had got immersed in the more managerial culture. I had had a little more first hand exposure to what was happening in private sector management … .

His overall aim was to move away from 'a health care system which was originally 1940s, based on the belief that armies of wartime type planners in a wartime planning structure could deliver a health care system by just getting money out of the Government' to:

> a system where purchasing becomes proper measurement of what's required, proper response to public interest and public need, proper thought about how

best you are going to provide the service. This should produce proper control with somebody really being able to make a decision about priorities in their locality, in their practice, their hospital. People at the sharp end should be deciding what sort of priority setting is going to be made, what kind of quantity and quality is going to be sought. The people running the Service, the medics, the nurses, will know what they are expected to deliver, know they've had a chance of arguing about why they are being expected to deliver this, and will do what they are asked to do in the public interest and not just pursue their private practice and their private enthusiasms. We made the basis of a modern health service ... .

This change of emphasis served another purpose in that it was more reassuring to staff groups and representatives of patients. This was noted by the *Financial Times* in an editorial published in June 1990, which commented:

During the past year, ministerial rhetoric has subtly changed. The original goals of NHS reform were couched in commercial language. There was much talk of the virtues of the 'internal market' in which hospitals would have to 'compete' for the custom of patients.

Much of this terminology has since been dropped. Districts have become 'commissioners' of care, GPs will be 'fundholders' and the different parts of the NHS will 'contract', rather than compete, with each other. Thus described, the reforms appear evolutionary rather than revolutionary, a natural progression from earlier efforts to improve efficiency.

The changes in terminology are sensible. It was stupid to alarm doctors needlessly with talk of markets and competition.

(*Financial Times*, 18 June 1990)

Clarke's ideas were shared by William Waldegrave, whose experience in government in the 1970s of the introduction of a new approach to research and development had convinced him of the value of a clear separation between purchasers and providers. Waldegrave also brought direct knowledge of industry to the job and it was this that led him to challenge the more naïve models of markets that informed some of the thinking behind the reforms. As he explained, in the NHS:

it isn't a real market. In a real market you have the capacity to say, 'I don't want to make this product at all. I'm just going to withdraw'. I mean Seagrams are turning themselves from a drinks company into a film making company. Dupont have just sold Amoco, their oil company. They don't want to be in oil any more, they want to be in biotechnology like everybody else. But you can't do that in the health service. It's about the supply of health care. And in a way if I'd been there right at the beginning I would have tried to introduce some of those concepts … .

In Waldegrave's view, 'we had got into a muddle between what was a metaphor and what was reality'. He saw part of his responsibility as to clarify the Government's intentions, and also to fulfil his brief of calming down the doctors by softening the language used to describe the reforms and by presenting them in a way that was more acceptable to the health professions. The priority given to *The Health of the Nation* stemmed from the same concern, offering an opportunity of shifting the terms of the debate away from the organisation of the NHS and towards issues that related more directly to the concerns of doctors and nurses.

Echoing these views, Virginia Bottomley recalled how 'I found the language of the market quite extraordinary … So throughout my time you almost never heard me use any of the jargon at all'. Bottomley's stance was reinforced by the importance she attached to the perceptions of NHS staff, many of whom she felt were not fully engaged with the Government's agenda – although she also recognised that presenting the reforms as being a clear break with the past may have been necessary to persuade an inherently conservative institution to take the changes seriously. She explained that:

I consistently took the view that the underlying ethos of the NHS was one of co-operation but the discipline of competition, of comparison, of evaluation, forced the system to look analytically and more self critically at their traditional ways of working. So tales were legion of consultants who did three operations a week as opposed to 20 operations a week, who spent time in Harley Street rather than the hospital. And when you cross-questioned people about what that meant in practice there was nobody who checked up … it's that sort of traditional working practice that would be changed by the distinctions between purchasing and providing, the secure commissioning of health and the delivery of health care, and if you called that an internal market it gave it a greater comprehensibility in political circles.

Stephen Dorrell shared the reluctance of his predecessors to use the language of competition. He recalled:

> I never used the term 'market' or 'competition' if I could avoid it, to be honest, because I think they are both words that carry with them so much baggage – and baggage that in the context of the health service minimises the support of what you are trying to do – that they are words best avoided.

While acknowledging that 'you can certainly describe the health service reforms we introduced as being the introduction of an internal market', Dorrell went on to explain his own thinking in terms remarkably similar to those used by Kenneth Clarke. This thinking centred on the idea that the reforms were first and foremost about strengthening management in the NHS. In his own words:

> my interpretation of the whole NHS management reform process was using modern management theory, not to deliver profits to shareholders, because there are no profits and no shareholders, but to deliver a good service to patients.

At the core of the reform process was delegation of responsibility for decisions in the same way that had happened in other organisations. As Dorrell argued:

> there's nothing unique to the health service about this, its frankly a commonplace of management schools over the last 30 years when asked the question of how you manage any large organisation, because that's where the person making the decision is most likely to understand its implications in terms of the people you are there to serve, and you give them authority to make decisions from the perspective of the health service context, the patient.

Dorrell also shared William Waldegrave's concerns about the way in which markets had been interpreted in the NHS. As he explained:

> if you go into the outside world where people compete in a business market place on a day-to-day basis, the concept that competition will also lead to partnership is something that again is a commonplace and you regularly find industrial companies that are working in joint ventures in one area and competing against each other in another. And so I think that the concept of competition as understood, or misunderstood, in the health service was very crude and one-dimensional.

It was for these reasons that Dorrell preferred to describe the changes taking place within the NHS as 'management reforms'. Not only did this phrase carry less risk of alienating NHS staff, but also it opened up more common ground with Labour's spokespersons on health issues as they sought to define their own policies. In this context, the White Paper, *The NHS: A Service with Ambitions*, was a stepping stone between the last phase of Conservative stewardship of the NHS and the return to power of Labour. A number of the themes in the White Paper were picked up by the Labour Government elected in 1997 as a new consensus on the future of the NHS began to emerge. To be sure, there remained important differences between the political parties on the direction of health policy but these were much less significant than had been the case almost a decade earlier.

London

The retreat from both the language of markets and the encouragement given to their use was related to the difficulty of allowing competition to operate in a public service like the NHS where ultimately politicians were accountable for what happened. Nowhere was this more apparent than in London, where the early signals thrown up by the market held out the prospect of considerable instability as purchasers considered moving contracts between providers. Most at risk were teaching hospitals in the centre of London, where costs were often higher than those of other providers and where purchasers therefore had a strong incentive to seek better value for money elsewhere. The emphasis placed on a steady state and a smooth take off was intended to limit the impact of competition in the first year and it soon became clear that the market would be managed or regulated by politicians and civil servants on a continuing basis to avoid harmful instability and to ensure that change was properly planned.

Margaret Thatcher acknowledged the salience of London in this process in her memoirs. The former Prime Minister recalled in the context of her review of the readiness of the NHS to implement the reforms in June 1990:

> *With all the political problems which the community charge was causing, we could not afford to run the risk of disruption in London and the possible closure of hospital wards because the Service was not capable of managing in the new more competitive environment. In the end, I decided against slowing down the reforms while urging that the closest attention should be paid to what was happening in London.*

(Thatcher, 1993, p.617)

To address the challenge of London, the Government decided to set up an inquiry in 1991 under Professor Sir Bernard Tomlinson to advise on how services should be organised. We have seen how successive health secretaries then worked through the consequences, in the process having to deal with a range of difficult choices. Commenting on this, William Waldegrave observed that:

> people appeared to think that markets meant that you didn't have to take decisions, that somehow everything was solved of its own accord and you hear bright young right wing columnists talking like that who have never been in business. Arnold Weinstock doesn't just sit there and the market miraculously closes the factories in Liverpool and opens them up somewhere else, he has to decide. And he does take risks. And you have to say, 'this is going to close and this is going to open, and this is where we are going to put resources'. You know you actually have to take decisions and this was rather like a huge conglomerate company in a sense saying, 'well, we've got resources all in the wrong places'. You can't just say, 'the market will decide. We'll just leave this factory until it goes bust in 20 years' time'. You have to decide.

Virginia Bottomley was the Secretary of State mainly responsible for responding to the Tomlinson Report and she was in no doubt that the market alone was insufficient to deal with the problems that existed in London. Like Waldegrave, Bottomley emphasised the political problems that resulted and the need to see through changes even if they were unpopular. And while Bottomley felt that considerable progress had been made in implementing these changes, Waldegrave was less certain. As he put it:

> there have been some gains. We have grouped the teaching hospitals. But there are still resources scattered all over the place. We still haven't got a proper primary health care system in large parts of London. We still haven't got psychiatric or geriatric beds adequately in London. We have got a lot of things we don't need and not got what we do need. So we haven't done that.

The experience of London demonstrated that the 'internal market' had become a politically managed market in which the combination of competitive pressures and political intervention was effective in achieving some change, but where the resistance of established institutions and local communities meant that the pace of change was often slow and the aspirations of the more ambitious reformers were disappointed. The political costs for those at the heart of the process were also high, as Virginia Bottomley acknowledged:

I had to go through quite a process of vilification which is not enjoyable for anybody and for somebody who was in fact so personally committed to the cause as I was, it was I suppose a bit harsh. But I think my family probably felt that as much or more than me.

She recognised that in dealing with these issues she could have involved the Prime Minister, who had offered to help, but:

I said 'no, no, you just keep away, if there are any problems in the NHS, you just say that's Virginia's responsibility'. So I'd learned my lesson from Nick Ridley which was if it's tough, the Secretary of State takes the decision, if it's easy you either give credit to the Prime Minister or you let your junior ministers do it. I had a stoical attitude – maybe I didn't have enough spin doctors explaining that this was my strategy.

The Health of the Nation

Work on the national health strategy started under Kenneth Clarke. He described how discussions on setting indicators and targets for improving the health of the population had been debated with the then chief medical officer, Donald Acheson, and had been picked up by Virginia Bottomley during her time as a junior minister in the face of scepticism and, ultimately, opposition from Clarke:

Virginia, who I'm a great fan of – Virginia was a good Minister of State when I was there running the social services side of the Department – was instantly sold on Donald's idea. She believed it, she was one of the architects. She was sold on the health indicators thing. I remember later in Cabinet meetings I was awkward. Afterwards I was one of the few members of the Government having just come out of Health saying that I thought that half of this was a complete waste of time and all we were doing was boosting the list of targets. If you hit them it would be nothing to do with the Government, and if you failed to hit them the Government would be blamed. The one I remember most clearly was unwanted pregnancies. What were the policies that were going to deliver quantitatively measured reductions in unwanted pregnancies? Didn't it have something to do with teenage parties more than government policy?

Stephen Dorrell confirmed this interpretation, remembering how Clarke 'was never very interested in it because he was concerned about the nanny state angle'. Bottomley, by contrast, had no such doubts. She explained:

I took the view that it was an essential underpinning. It gave sense to everything we were doing. It was an agenda item that clinicians could identify with. It gave them something positive to say. Doctors, nurses, others were never going to say they loved fundholding, trusts or purchasing because the language and the whole concept, the structural change, was only ever going to turn a few on, but this was about health, coalitions and partnerships so … this was something to seize on. Peter [Bottomley] had done the drink driving campaign and I have always been pretty against smoking, and I never worried about being nannying.

Clarke related this different approach to underlying political differences:

I think the difference between the Social Democrat and, I'm not a Christian Democrat but a right of centre Conservative like me, is if you are a Social Democrat you think there's a political answer to everything. If you are a Conservative like me, you think there's a limit to the size of government, there's a limit to the role of government, and the idea that government action can, for example, reduce the number of unwanted pregnancies in the country strikes me as somewhat unlikely.

Others thought there was a simpler explanation of Clarke's opposition. William Waldegrave, who revived the strategy after taking office, remembered that Clarke felt that preventative medicine was just 'a lot of fashionable claptrap', and in any case, 'He [Clarke] had his own habits of a lifetime to think about!' Waldegrave was persuaded of the value of the strategy for the same reasons as Bottomley and he was instrumental in publishing the consultative document on which *The Health of the Nation* White Paper was based. Waldegrave felt that it was:

a relative success having got that launched against a great deal of cynicism from my predecessor who at that point became rather right wing and said, 'this is all a limitation on freedom'.

Elaborating on the divisions within the Government, Bottomley recalled that after the 1992 general election 'I went to a fearful meeting – a Cabinet committee meeting – one of my first ones in the Cabinet, where there was a major attempt to mug the whole process'. Her opponents felt that it was 'antipathetic to the free market Tory style' and she recalled how 'I fought like a tigress to get that White Paper out'. John Major's support was important in overcoming disagreements within the Cabinet but Bottomley recognised that 'within my Party it was never to have much more life. We got it there, it was part of the framework, people could use it who wanted to, but it was never going to really take off in a noisier way'. Stephen Dorrell initiated a review of progress with the strategy to coincide with the fifth anniversary of its publication but as this fell beyond the 1997 general election he did not attach particular priority to it. Dorrell's own approach was summarised as 'I didn't want to walk away from it but I didn't particularly want to develop it either'. The ambivalence within the Government to *The Health of the Nation* helps to explain research evidence that the impact of the strategy within the NHS was limited (Department of Health, 1998).

Primary care

Fundholding was instrumental in putting primary care at the heart of the NHS agenda, particularly in the latter part of the period 1988–97. This found expression in Virginia Bottomley's policy of developing a 'primary care led NHS', announced in 1994, which was designed to offer a wider range of fundholding options to GPs as well as to encourage GPs who chose not to become fundholders to work with health authorities to realise the benefits of fundholding (as the Government saw it) in other ways. Stephen Dorrell took this policy a stage further in resolving the dispute on out-of-hours arrangements with GPs and using the opportunity this created to undertake a review of primary care arrangements as a whole.

Dorrell explained that the background to this initiative was the survey carried out by the General Medical Services Committee (GMSC) of the BMA and the concerns this had identified among GPs. His aim was to take discussion of these concerns out of the context of negotiations between the Government and the BMA and this eventually emerged as the 'listening exercise' in which the Minister of State for Health, Gerald Malone, undertook a round of consultation with family doctors designed to set out a new way forward for primary care. Dorrell described the listening exercise as 'a sort of flanking manoeuvre building on the momentum we had achieved in out-of-hours', and intended to appeal not only to 'leading edge GPs' who were enthusiastic fundholders but also the 'middle range' of GPs who were concerned about their working arrangements and where there was an opportunity for the Government to connect with these GPs and demonstrate that it wanted to make a positive difference.

The listening exercise resulted in the publication of a consultation paper on primary care in 1996 and two White Papers setting out the Government's proposals. A wide variety of ideas were contained in these documents. One of the key themes was that there should be greater flexibility in employment arrangements for GPs and other family practitioners. This included the option of salaried employment for GPs and locally negotiated practice-based contracts. The White Papers also proposed that NHS resources should be used more flexibly, for example to enable funds for hospital and community health services to be allocated to primary care where GPs and nurses took on a wider range of responsibilities. The NHS (Primary Care) Act 1997, which was passed with the support of the Opposition parties shortly before the general election, provided the statutory framework to implement these proposals. The bipartisan support for the Act symbolised the emergence of a new consensus on health policy.

Reflecting on developments in primary care, Dorrell maintained that his greatest achievement was:

> to have persuaded a Tory Government, in the last session of Parliament before a general election, to table an NHS Bill, the effect of which was, without throwing out the existing successful structures of primary care, to introduce a new alternative structure for general practice which reflected the purchaser/provider arrangements which had been introduced with such high political drama in 1990.

This was especially so in that:

> the logic that is there in the Primary Care Act is the logic that to some extent lies behind some of what Frank Dobson is now doing, and will prove to be an important step in further developing primary care within the NHS.

To this extent, GP fundholding, which was often perceived as the wild card in a set of reforms designed to address the funding problems of acute hospitals, set off a train of events that were unplanned but which were to have significant implications in the longer term. This illustrates how policy can often have unanticipated effects and lead to change going well beyond that which was originally intended.

Public expenditure and private finance

Negotiating additional resources for the NHS was an important issue for all four health secretaries but was particularly salient around the time of general elections. William Waldegrave and Stephen Dorrell were in office in 1992 and 1997 respectively and they recalled in some detail the course taken in the public expenditure survey (PES) process. Waldegrave observed:

> *I was in the position that all secretaries of state are always in just when elections are coming up, which is that the management say that by a strange coincidence everything is going to grind to a halt a week before the election unless huge sums of money are produced.*

Waldegrave used his bargaining position and the support of John Major for the NHS to extract a favourable settlement:

> *I did take it right down to the wire knowing very clearly that I had a very strong position and that Chris Patten and John Major were not going to take risks with the health service in the run-up to the election and both of them anyway were fundamental supporters of the Service. I think in fact we probably got more money than we needed which is the irrational thing but I'm very happy to say that Duncan [Nichol] was quite equal to salting a lot of it away in reserves for future years.*

Stephen Dorrell reported having a harder time persuading the Treasury to provide adequate funding for the NHS in the run-up to the 1997 election. He felt part of the reason may have been having to negotiate with Treasury ministers who had experience in the Department of Health:

> *There was a lot of resistance, quite serious resistance, in the Government to Health getting money along the lines that the health service is never going to win us any votes anyway, and we've heard from health secretaries before. And I'm never sure whether it was an advantage or a disadvantage that both Ken Clarke and William Waldegrave had been Health Secretary before me and I think they both felt that they knew where the bodies were buried and they were not going to be rolled over by all these arguments that they'd heard before because they'd used them before.*

In these circumstances, Dorrell made it clear that he would have resigned rather than acquiesce to an unacceptable settlement. Faced with the prospect of a winter beds crisis that would have made his position 'unsustainable', he felt:

I might just as well go in a blaze of glory at the time of the PES argument as become a sort of, in the nicest sense of the word, the Douglas Hogg of Health, during the January and February before an election.

In this PES round, Dorrell described how he tried to introduce a more systematic approach to the assessment of expenditure requirements by focusing on the main drivers of change instead of the detailed components. He was willing to accept the settlement on offer because of his commitment to shift public resources for health care from capital to revenue. This was possible because of his enthusiasm for the private finance initiative (PFI) as an alternative to Treasury funding of capital schemes. Dorrell's own experience in the Treasury had made him aware of the potential role of PFI in government as a whole, and on his return to the Department of Health he gave priority to promoting its use. Although progress in implementing major PFI schemes in the NHS was slow before the 1997 general election, the foundations were laid for a major expansion of this approach thereafter.

The NHS Executive

One of Kenneth Clarke's bequests to William Waldegrave was a decision to move the headquarters of the NHS Executive to Leeds. Clarke explained the rationale for this:

The culture of the Department, the headquarters, struck me as hopelessly centralising and bureaucratic. There are people around in the Department of Health with a lot of very good qualities, public health and other things, but it's still too big. God knows what they all do, but there are core things with very dedicated people who can do well. I wanted the management running the system to be away from Whitehall, to be less politicised, to be more autonomous, able to implement the reforms without the inevitable constant pressure to water it down, not to do anything for the moment, to delay it, to not upset the BMA, not upset the royal colleges, not upset the RCN which I thought was the ethos here.

Characteristically, Clarke recalled that:

There had been a row about this because nobody wanted to go to Leeds. Officials, even the smallest government agency, if you asked them where they wanted to go, say, 'Oxford Street or Whitehall', so nobody wanted to go.

He persisted in the face of opposition and eventually got his way. Waldegrave remembered having lunch with Clarke on taking up office at La Poule au Pot – 'our favourite restaurant' – and being told by Clarke that:

> one of the things he had most helpfully done was – just so I needn't bother about it – was to sign a piece of paper the day before saying that the Health Service Executive should move to Leeds. So I didn't need to worry about that.

Although not a major issue, Waldegrave felt in retrospect that he should have reversed the decision because:

> it was, I believe, a silly idea actually. The idea that if you put everybody together a long way away they would all sort of behave in a more entrepreneurial way – all it meant was that they wasted a huge amount of time on railway trains and it wasted a lot of money and time.

The significance of this issue lies in the willingness of a secretary of state to act in this way in the hope and belief that creating a physical distance between that part of the Department of Health responsible for overseeing implementation of the reforms and the policy networks in which decisions were taken would alter the balance of power and create more support for the policies the Government was pursuing. Fundamentally, Clarke was seeking to change the culture of the Department of Health and believed that the organisational separation of the NHS Executive within the Department, coupled with its geographical separation, would lend support to the managerial changes taking place within the NHS itself. This relates to the much bigger question of the world in which health secretaries function and the sources of advice and information available to them. If, as Kenneth Clarke was suggesting, the Department of Health was inclined to favour a quiet life in which priority was given to appeasing major interest groups rather than promoting new policies that might prove controversial, then where did the secretaries of state turn for support and what kind of world do they occupy? We go on to discuss this question in Chapter 3.

Summary: The policy agenda

Our review of the policy agenda during this period indicates that while implementing the internal market remained a priority, other policies also became important. These policies included *The Health of the Nation*, the Patient's Charter and the reform of primary care. To some extent, this reflected the concern of politicians to address issues of importance to NHS staff and the public, and to some extent it arose out of the concern of politicians themselves to make their mark on the NHS. Whatever the explanation, the effect was the same: the size and scope of the health policy agenda became more complex, with issues that initially appeared as significant being supplemented, and in some cases overtaken, by other concerns.

If policy overload was one consequence, then policy incoherence was another. Not only did the NHS lack the capacity to deliver all the objectives set by politicians during this period, with the result that there was often a gap between intention and action (Department of Health, 1998), but also to outside observers the connection between policies promoted at different points in time was not always apparent. And while Virginia Bottomley, among others, made strenuous efforts to explain the Government's consistency of purpose (Bottomley, 1995), the degree of dissonance between policies driven by a belief in competition and those requiring effective planning and co-ordination became greater. Policy development during this period demonstrated the inherent messiness at the heart of government as politicians strove to muddle through as best they could (Lindblom, 1959).

Chapter 3

People

In this chapter we draw together the evidence from the accounts of the health secretaries in relation to the world in which they worked. The chapter begins by describing how they saw the job and goes on to discuss the sources of support and advice available to them.

The job

The complexity of the role of secretary of state was emphasised by William Waldegrave. He described it as 'one of the biggest jobs for any government minister' given the size of the budget and the direct responsibility of the secretary of state for everything that happens in the NHS. The paradox this created was that 'it's the most horrible job politically of any in Whitehall and the most satisfying and interesting and challenging and powerful of many top jobs in terms of what you do'. The horror of the job derived from the intense media and public interest in the NHS and the risks for ministers and governments if things went wrong; the satisfaction arose out of the opportunity to really make a difference, which in the case of the NHS reforms stemmed from the fact that 'we got the reforms underway and we created the basis for long-term stability in the sense that the wisest heads of the thinking people on the centre-left knew that this wasn't all nonsense and some kind of consensus began'.

Virginia Bottomley communicated the same sense of a love/hate relationship with the job. For her, 'I just felt this was the job of all jobs I was interested in, I would want to have done, and I had this wonderful opportunity to do it and therefore it was a real sense of wanting to get the decisions right'. Bottomley added that throughout her time at the Department 'I … regarded myself really like an executive chairman. I felt enormously responsible and 24-hours-a-day concerned about the NHS'. The pressures of the job were particularly evident in relation to London and Bottomley described how she felt that coping with these pressures was the price she had to pay to bring about necessary changes in service configuration.

Former health secretaries Virginia Bottomley and Kenneth Clarke.

The experience that politicians brought with them was particularly important in influencing their approach to the job. Kenneth Clarke emphasised that his time as Minister of State for Health had shaped his own thinking. This meant that 'I knew the health service inside out, and I had strong views on it and I reckoned I knew more about management than half the people I was discussing it with'. William Waldegrave brought experience of government and industry and this informed his approach, with its emphasis on improving the management of the NHS and introducing change gradually. Virginia Bottomley's background in social services meant that she had worked in one of the sectors for which she was responsible and the involvement of various family members in health care was also important. She explained that:

> *I had done nothing but think about the NHS for the last 25 years – I mean my every waking day, all my life has been surrounded by doctors and I think 17 of my relations are doctors and many of my friends were involved – they were nurses or health managers and a number of academics.*

Stephen Dorrell combined experience in his family business with a period as a junior minister in the Department of Health and this meant that he brought the same managerial instincts to the job as Clarke and Waldegrave, as well as their commitment to the NHS model as the preferred way of organising health services.

The style with which the job was done depended greatly on the individuals appointed to it. We have noted already the contrast between Kenneth Clarke's assertive promotion of the reforms and William Waldegrave's more emollient approach. There was an equally striking contrast between Virginia Bottomley and Stephen Dorrell. The Economist commented upon this shortly after Dorrell took up office: 'So he works from a comfy armchair instead of Mrs Bottomley's big table. So he issues fewer press releases. So he has declared his Department a statistics-free zone'. The same article commented that 'Mrs Bottomley's worst fault is not insincerity but insecurity. It drove her from bed at dawn to master every known fact about the NHS. It produced her missionary zeal' (*The Economist*, 12 August 1995).

By implication, Dorrell was altogether more relaxed and less anxious to counter every hint of criticism with his own version of events. For her part, Bottomley argued that her training as a social scientist led her to support her case with facts and evidence whenever possible. She also took seriously Margaret Thatcher's advice to take every opportunity to explain the

Government's policies. In this respect, she felt she was setting an example for people in the NHS to follow, particularly in communicating with the public on the rationale of change.

To make this point is to highlight the importance that the secretaries of state attached to the media in reporting NHS matters. The role of the media was emphasised particularly by Bottomley and Waldegrave, who spent much of their time responding to the press as well as trying to influence the line taken by the media in its coverage of the NHS. This included seeking to keep the NHS out of the headlines alongside action to convey the Government's policies in a positive light. Regional newspapers like the *Evening Standard* in London could be just as significant as the national media in this context. To extend the story beyond the period covered in this book, the importance of the media was not lost on the Labour Government elected in 1997, whose efforts at news management were reflected in Virginia Bottomley's observation that her case for change in the NHS might have been more successful if she had employed more spin doctors.

The Department

The secretaries of state were able to call on various sources of support in dealing with the demands of the job. Particularly important were other ministerial colleagues within the Department and civil servants at the 'top of the office'. Among these civil servants, the chief executive of the NHS (Duncan Nichol followed by Alan Langlands), the chief medical officer (Donald Acheson followed by Kenneth Calman) and the permanent secretary (Chris France followed by Graham Hart) were not surprisingly seen as the most significant. There was also the support available from private office and special advisers. William Waldegrave placed particular value on the advice he received from the Policy Board, whose members comprised non-executives from the NHS and business, as well as civil servants from the top of the office.

Virginia Bottomley elaborated on the relationship between civil servants, distinguishing between the role of the permanent secretary as 'the Whitehall warrior' sorting out issues in Whitehall and Westminster, and the chief executive of the NHS (later known as the chief executive of the NHS Executive) who, if something came up, 'had to be an excellent witness to the Chancellor or the Prime Minister'. The chief medical officer she described as 'the go-between between the professions and the Department', a role which quite often gave rise to 'a conflict of loyalties'. Bottomley recalled how she used to have Wednesday morning meetings with top of the office staff to work though issues and to ensure a consistent approach.

The contribution of other senior officials was acknowledged as being significant throughout this period. NHS Executive directors such as the deputy chief executive (Peter Griffiths followed by Andrew Foster), the director of finance (Sheila Masters), and the director of research and development (Michael Peckham) were mentioned by name, as were such counterparts in the wider Department as the deputy secretary (Strachan Heppell) and the chief economic adviser (Clive Smee). Other civil servants with particular policy responsibilities were also reported to have played an important role in relation to issues such as primary care and the national health strategy, although their contribution varied depending on the policy agenda at the time. The private secretaries who served the health secretaries acted as a bridge between politicians and the Department and could be a source of policy ideas in their own right.

The secretaries of state were not always successful in putting in place the support systems they felt they needed within the Department. Kenneth Clarke, for example, recalled how on his appointment he had a struggle with the permanent secretary to assemble a team of younger officials to work with him on the NHS Review:

> I had 6000 officials most of whom I had no idea what on earth they did, and I remember having great difficulty getting a team together because I was told nobody was free. They were all too busy doing God knows what. In the end I did get a very high powered team of officials in their 30s with whom I could sit and have long natters of the kind I'm having with you. I think I always used to choose them. We could sketch out ideas, we could throw them around and then they'd draft the papers.

Once these initial difficulties had been overcome, Clarke reported that he received valuable support from his officials, a view echoed by his successors.

Special advisers tended to play a complementary role to civil servants, being less involved in the development of policy and more concerned to maintain lines of political communication to the Party in Westminster and in the country. William Waldegrave noted that advisers were particularly important at the time of the 1992 general election in linking with Party activists in the country and ensuring that the Conservatives' case was represented effectively to the media. Unlike civil servants, special advisers come and go with politicians, and they were reported as serving a number of purposes including writing speeches and acting as a sounding board for ideas. They also provided a link to organisations like the Conservative Medical Society and from time to time worked with officials in testing the political implications of policy proposals generated within the Department. The contribution of these advisers was supplemented by the input of elder statesmen like Sir Roy Griffiths, who continued to play a part in advising secretaries of state and prime ministers on the development of health policy after his work on the general management and community care inquiries.

The NHS

Beyond the Department, the secretaries of state received support from people in the NHS. After the advice given by civil servants and fellow ministers, this was regarded as the most important input to their thinking. The chairmen of regional health authorities were seen as particularly valuable in this respect. Kenneth Clarke recalled that:

> *Norman Fowler and I had great strength in the RHAs when we were there before. We used to call the regional chairmen our health cabinet. And we greatly depended on them to discuss things with because they were in the regions, were the only people we'd got trying to sell the merits of all this and give us feedback, and sell it to the Service. They were not closely involved in the detail. I tried everything out on them. One or two of them fed in good ideas and were extremely useful ears and eyes, keeping the show on the road, stopping it grinding to a halt while the controversy was going on.*

Similarly, Virginia Bottomley remembered that 'the people I had a lot of time for were the regional chairmen'. She described the chairmen as:

> *the people who I found sound, committed, constructive, whether it was Don Wilson with his, 'you want waiting lists, I'll give you waiting lists. If you want women, I'll give you women' but he delivered. Rennie Fritchie brought a new, different style with interest and understanding of the women issues, and later William Wells, shrewd, tough, able.*

William Waldegrave also noted the role played by regional chairmen, commenting that they:

could be very useful in taking some of the strain off the Secretary of State by dealing with local and regional media, etc. They were rather like French prefects.

Waldegrave added that the co-existence of regional chairmen and non-executive members of the Policy Board led to 'some tension between the two' because 'effectively, there were two alternative senior management structures'. And while the logic of a modern system of corporate governance for the NHS pointed to the removal of regional chairmen, their value to politicians meant that they continued to perform a key function even after the abolition of regional health authorities in 1996.

Bottomley did not rely only on regional chairmen. Every summer she would spend time in each region meeting health authority and trust chairmen and hearing their views. On these occasions she would say, 'please tell me the three things that you are doing well, and what you think the three problems are ... I probably had more information than anybody about what people were thinking'. Bottomley also saw an important part of the job as keeping in touch with NHS staff, 'checking that the agenda driven by the politicians was relevant to the issues experienced by people working in the Service'.

Kenneth Clarke felt the same, recalling that 'Within the health service, I soaked up the views and the reactions of ordinary practitioners as much as I could'. Stephen Dorrell's perception was that 'the health service is such a large organisation it has its own private version of the chattering classes'. Dorrell felt it was important to establish a relationship with the NHS chattering classes 'so that they understood what your basic objectives were in the areas that interested and concerned them. It was actually an important part of the health service politics, never mind the capital "p" politics'.

Much of the time of secretaries of state is spent at official functions and dinners where there are opportunities to gather intelligence about what is happening in the NHS. Virginia Bottomley recalled 'always sitting at dinner listening to my neighbours. So, if you go to a dinner, you spend two hours sitting next to the president of the college, or the head of the IHSM'. These conversations contributed to her thinking and the same applied to Stephen Dorrell, who remembered:

quite often what used to happen was that I sat next to somebody at dinner or something and after a couple of minutes talking about holidays and wives and children I used to find it much more interesting then to talk about their ideas

Stephen Dorrell MP receives a petition from a supporter of the Save Solihull
Hospital group, 1996.

*about the health service. And if I found somebody who was saying something
interesting, I'd ask them whether it had been written down ... if you are sat
next to somebody for an hour, an hour-and-a-half, and they are talking about
their area of expertise, you don't actually then need to go away and read it
because you've got something out of it which you can then go away and feed in
and ask officials, 'well suppose we did this, what would be the result?'*

The other source of NHS input derived from constituents whose views were
valued and individuals who themselves made a point of seeking to inform or
influence secretaries of state. William Waldegrave recalled how his own GP
and the chief executive of an NHS trust in his constituency had been
important in this way, while Virginia Bottomley was able to reel off a list of
names of people with whom she had talked. These people included a number
of chairmen and chief executives of NHS trusts whom she met or
communicated with in other ways in the course of testing her own ideas and
thinking. She also, to use Stephen Dorrell's phrase, maintained contact with
the NHS's chattering classes, remembering:

*I saw a whole great raft of people who used to come and see me ... I used to
talk to Robert Maxwell, I talked to Julia Neuberger, I talked to Margaret Jay,
I talked to Claire Rayner, I talked to – I was really interested in what people
had to say – I talked to John Spiers, I talked to Roy Lilley ... I talked to ... the
waiting list man ... John Yates.*

Professional organisations

Organisations representing health professionals, especially doctors, figured
prominently in the reflections of the secretaries of state. Most often mentioned
were the BMA and the royal medical colleges. These organisations occupied a
dominant place in the thinking of the health secretaries, whose policies and
actions were rarely formulated without thought being given to how they would
be received by the medical profession and its representatives. Kenneth Clarke's
antipathy to the BMA derived from his diagnosis that the NHS:

*was dominated by its interest groups, by its trade unions, by professional
employees and hardly any regard at all was paid either to patient priorities, nor
was anyone stepping back to decide 'well, how could you run a health service
based on these principles in the medium to long term'.*

Relationships between the Government and the BMA reached a low point during Clarke's term of office and improved only slowly thereafter.

William Waldegrave felt that he was helped in his job of calming down the doctors by having Jeremy Lee-Potter as head of the BMA at that time. Waldegrave described Lee-Potter as 'a friend and a very moderate man' who suffered at the hands of his BMA colleagues for his moderation: a view confirmed by Lee-Potter's own memoirs (Lee-Potter, 1997). Virginia Bottomley shared Clarke's view that the BMA was essentially a trade union and she felt that the BMA was 'disappointingly short term and lacking in depth in the issues they raised'.

Stephen Dorrell fared rather better than his predecessors because by the time he took up office the sound and the fury that had attended the launch of the NHS reforms had dissipated. Moreover, Dorrell displayed a degree of tactical acumen in his dealings with the General Medical Services Committee of the BMA by initiating a review of primary care that addressed many of the concerns of GPs. He was able to do this because by the time of his appointment both the style and the substance of the health policy debate had shifted significantly.

The royal colleges were generally viewed more positively than the BMA. Kenneth Clarke recalled that the presidents of the colleges of psychiatrists and general practitioners were 'very good' and 'very supportive'. Similarly, Virginia Bottomley remembered that 'some of the royal college people I took seriously', although she noted that the colleges were 'somewhat devoid of the reality of high politics'. In Bottomley's view there was an unhelpful schism between the BMA, which looked after the interests of doctors as health services staff, and the colleges with their involvement in education and medical standards. The leadership of the medical profession suffered because no one organisation brought these agendas together, although she recalled valuing the advice she received from the president of the General Medical Council and the head of the Postgraduate Medical Federation. In a different way, Kenneth Clarke emphasised the key role played by Tony Trafford (a renal specialist) when he was appointed, albeit briefly, as a junior minister in the Department, particularly in acting as 'an emissary to the doctors'.

By contrast, relationships with other health professions did not attract the same amount of comment, although the role of the RCN in representing nurses was acknowledged, as was the advice offered by its general secretary, Christine Hancock.

Think tanks and academics

One of the features of health policy during this period was the attempt by think tanks to shape and influence the debate. This was most apparent during the Ministerial Review but think tanks continued to take an active interest in health policy in later years. The testimony of the secretaries of state is that the work of these bodies did not exert much influence. For example, when Kenneth Clarke was asked about the significance of the Adam Smith Institute, the Centre for Policy Studies and similar groups, his reaction was a blunt 'They didn't have any influence on me'. Similarly, Virginia Bottomley recalled 'I don't think they had a lot to say by then. They'd done their best or their worst'.

Rather more important was the King's Fund, which William Waldegrave felt was 'very influential in relation to London', not least because of its analysis of the weaknesses of London's health services (King's Fund, 1992). Virginia Bottomley was more critical of the King's Fund, arguing that having made the case for change in London, the Fund failed to give the Government credit for acting to achieve change. Her frustration reached the point where:

> I became exasperated by the King's Fund because I'd wanted the King's Fund to become an NHS management college and I would have worked hard to deliver that. But they consistently produced reports ... at key political times in the cycle, which were ill judged, provocatively presented, evidently playing politics.

Academics were reported as having had a role to play at various stages. Most obviously and significantly, there was the influence during the Ministerial Review of Alain Enthoven whose ideas when originally published had appeared to fall on stony ground. In the event, Enthoven's thinking was to prove an escape route when the Review reached the end of a cul-de-sac on alternative funding options and decided instead to explore ways of strengthening the delivery of health services. At a later stage, the research of academics at the LSE was seen to have been valuable, reinforcing the commitment to GP fundholding and providing support from an unlikely source for the Government's plans.

The contribution of academics was described variously. Virginia Bottomley used the word 'mercenaries' to refer to 'the likes of you [the author] and Alan Maynard', whom she felt 'actually are very influential'. William Waldegrave felt the Department of Health was 'rather well served' in this regard with 'four or five serious contributors who were not just taking a party ticket on any of this'. Waldegrave drew a parallel with the Foreign Office, seeing the Department of Health as 'the only other department I can think of where there are serious people inside the circuit who know as much as the professionals'. All the secretaries of state interviewed were at pains to emphasise that academics writing from an independent and research base had more influence than individuals who were perceived at the time as being influential, such as the Gloucestershire GP, Clive Froggatt, later convicted of offences under the Dangerous Drugs Act.

Parliament

In emphasising the role of individuals and organisations outside government, it is important not to overlook the continuing influence of Parliament. While not the most significant consideration in the minds of the health secretaries, the work of select committees, together with the contribution of individual MPs during debates and at question time, could not be ignored. It was through these channels that Parliamentary accountability was discharged. The fact that the Government enjoyed a majority throughout this period meant that the health secretaries could be certain of support in Parliament for their legislation but they could still come under pressure from MPs pressing constituency matters and from select committees on policy issues. Special advisers were, as we have noted, a way of maintaining communication with backbench MPs in Parliament, but personal contact between health secretaries and their Parliamentary colleagues was also important from time to time, especially when ministers were felt to be under pressure.

Thinking time

A strong impression to emerge from the reflections of the health secretaries was the limited time available to them to read and think independently on the issues with which they were confronted. This meant that there was little scope for testing out ideas. Virginia Bottomley recalled having only 'one free evening in three weeks' and she explained that she brought her ideas together in the process of writing speeches because 'speech time was thinking time' and:

> When I did a speech I'd run it like a university seminar ... I'd try and get the people who knew about it and I'd get somebody from the clinical side, and one of the officials, and I'd use the whole process of some of the big speeches to think through where I wanted to go.

Bottomley likened the process of speech writing to doing a university essay, compiling a lot of articles and using them to structure her thoughts. Similarly, Stephen Dorrell recalled that he would occasionally ask for reading lists and articles or recommended texts from the Department. Also, he would protect time at weekends and in between meetings to think through the issues. His coping strategy was:

> to consciously step out of my role as a minister to the maximum extent. I'd never have the ministerial car driving me round the country ... if you are in a car for three hours on a Friday night you've got a bit of thinking time, so I think that's ... part of the answer. It's not to be a minister seven days a week [but] to be a minister for four or five days a week but then to be a political/private citizen.

This was again where special advisers had a contribution to make when they worked effectively, although the value of these advisers in practice was reported as varying enormously. Yet in making these points, the pressure of events needs to be emphasised. The health secretaries often found themselves forced to make decisions and formulate announcements at short notice and were able to exercise control of their world only to a limited extent. In view of this, it was not surprising that they relied on civil servants for support, as proximity meant that officials were well placed to offer advice and the familiarity developed over a period of time created an interdependency that others found difficult to match. Thinking time was the exception not the rule and most decisions were less the result of careful calculation than a response to the incessant demands of the job and the advice of officials.

Summary: The world of health secretaries

The picture that emerges is of a world in which secretaries of state rely first and foremost on their own experience and instincts, supplemented by discussions with ministerial colleagues and civil servants. Views from within the NHS are perceived to be important and this applies as much to the views of ordinary staff as to the opinions of chairmen and senior managers. Think tanks were seen as less influential than academics and researchers, and special advisers could also be valuable, although this was not always the case. The lobbying of professional organisations was a constant consideration in the minds of the health secretaries. At some points, politicians were prepared to override the views of these organisations, while at others they went to some length to carry them along and to anticipate their response to policy initiatives.

The pressure under which health secretaries work is self-evident, with little time available for independent reading and reflection and much of the job focusing on responding to issues and crises as they arise. This meant that time spent at social functions and dinners was important in offering exposure to people and ideas outside the Department. The secretaries of state also used their own networks and contacts to test out ideas. In this respect, the 'chattering classes' of the NHS were seen as an important grouping. The thinking developed in this way was sometimes refined through discussions with family members who were involved in health care.

The impression that this creates is of formal and structured processes of policy development within government being supplemented by relatively random and much less structured processes outside government. It is out of this 'policy soup' (Kingdon, 1995) that decisions eventually emerge. We now go on in Chapter 4 to analyse how our findings relate to the literature on policy-making.

Chapter 4

Analysis

In seeking to make sense of the research reported here, the work of analysts who have sought to describe and explain the dynamics of policy-making from a political science perspective will be drawn on. This perspective offers a range of concepts relevant to understanding the experience of health secretaries between 1988 and 1997. In particular, it enables us to relate the accounts of the politicians concerned to debates within the political science literature on the distribution of power within government, the relationship between government and outside interests, and the way in which policy agendas are set. This chapter of the book summarises relevant aspects of this literature and then reviews what the data presented so far tell us about health policy-making during this period.

Concepts and theories

Political scientists have progressively moved away from descriptions of the formal institutions of government and have focused instead on studying behaviour and relationships between institutions and other interests. Among these interests, the functioning of pressure groups has received particular attention. This is because the growth of government in the past century has been accompanied by the proliferation of groups seeking to influence what governments do. In this way, the established channels of representative democracy have been supplemented by other forms of representation.

The place occupied by pressure groups in Britain exemplifies the 'collectivist theory of representation' (Beer, 1969, p.70), which legitimises a much greater role for groups than earlier theories of representation that focused on the role of elections and political parties. As Beer notes, as government sought to manage the economy it was led to bargain with organised groups of producers, in particular worker and employer associations. Similarly the evolution of the welfare state provoked action by organised groups of consumers of services, such as tenants, parents and patients. The activities of these groups were supplemented by organisations representing the providers of public services, including teachers and doctors. Relationships between groups and government vary but it is the producer and provider groups that tend to have the closest contacts and greatest degree of influence.

Students of politics have pointed to the growth of pressure groups in support of the pluralist theory of democracy. This theory argues that policy-making is relatively open and fluid, with resources to influence government widely distributed and with many groups in a position to shape policy outcomes. According to pluralists, no group is without power and, equally, no group is dominant. In essence, any group can exert some influence if it is sufficiently determined and skilful in its use of the political process. The pluralists' explanation of this is that the sources of power – like money, information and expertise – are distributed non-cumulatively. Essentially, then, in a pluralist political system power is fragmented and diffused, and the basic picture presented is of a political market place where what a group achieves depends on its resources and its decibel rating.

The pluralists' position has been challenged by critics who contend that power is more concentrated than this theory allows. These critics draw on the research of Eckstein (1960) and others to suggest that corporatism is a better description than pluralism of the relationship between government and groups like the British Medical Association (BMA). The contention of corporatists is that producer groups are better placed than other organisations to influence policy and have been closely incorporated into the machinery of government. This applies particularly in the field of economic policy where trades unions and employers' associations have in effect become 'governing institutions' (Middlemas, 1979, p.372). Cawson (1982) has extended the analysis of corporatism to the area of social policy, arguing that pressure groups representing the providers of public services like health care are in a qualitatively different position to other organisations because of their ability to work closely with policy-makers. While some writers argue that corporatism has replaced pluralism, in Cawson's analysis the two co-exist, with consumer groups in a less privileged position than producer groups.

The work of both pluralists and corporatists has been questioned by researchers who have argued that neither term offers an adequate account of the relationships that have developed between government and outside interests. These researchers have focused their attention instead on the emergence of policy networks that link government departments and pressure groups in different ways. Policy networks take a variety of forms, a key distinction being between *policy communities* involving relatively stable relationships between a small number of actors, and *issue networks*, which are more flexible and permeable (Marsh and Rhodes, 1992b). Policy communities are sometimes equated with 'iron triangles' in which ministers and civil servants develop close contacts with significant client pressure groups and work with these groups both in the development of policy and in its implementation. The concept of iron triangles was developed in studies of government in the USA, though the rigidities it implies have been questioned by researchers who seek to reassert an interpretation in keeping with the pluralist tradition by pointing to the importance of more fluid issue networks (Heclo, 1978).

In drawing attention to the policy network perspective, it should be noted that it is rare for policy communities or issue networks to exist in pure form. Empirical studies have described a wide range of arrangements, including in the health field the existence of both iron triangles and issue networks (Haywood and Hunter, 1982). Among other things, this highlights variations within policy sectors and the need to avoid the application of general theories and concepts that do not allow for these variations. It is also important to recognise that while policy communities tend to be stable, they may be affected by macro changes in the economic environment and by the political ideology of the government in power. As far as the latter is concerned, government is not simply the referee regulating the struggle for influence between pressure groups, as some of the early versions of pluralist theory contended, but has its own views and preferences and from time to time these may challenge the stability and consensus that develops between pressure groups and civil servants within policy communities.

To make this point is to underscore another relevant strand in the literature, namely the role of politicians and civil servants in policy-making. The influence of these actors has been emphasised by researchers who have sought to correct the impression created in some studies that pressure groups have become the main influence on policy outcomes. Rather, it is argued that policy communities involve bargaining and negotiation between pressure groups and government departments, where actors are dependent on each other. Politicians and civil servants are influential in this process, even though they may be constrained by the need to access the specialist knowledge of pressure groups and secure their co-operation in implementation. From this perspective, 'state centred' explanations of policy-making need to receive as much prominence as 'society centred' explanations.

An important argument in this context is that power in policy communities is more than a zero-sum game (Smith, 1993). Particularly in fields like health policy, it is argued that governments actively seek to incorporate those pressure groups whose support is needed to deliver policy objectives. In return, these groups gain influence and resources, notwithstanding the existence of conflicts between government and groups on some issues. By working together, the actors in policy communities may enhance each other's power, for example by winning more resources from the Treasury. In the process, these actors strengthen their position in relation to other policy communities and to politicians and civil servants elsewhere in government.

As these comments suggest, the internal workings of government, including the relationship between ministers and civil servants, also shape policy outcomes. A landmark example of work that addressed this issue was Heclo and Wildavsky's 1974 study of life in the Whitehall village. Like the literature on policy networks, this study emphasised the importance of relationships between civil servants during the public expenditure planning round and the community of interest that grew up during the process. Relationships in this community were governed by implicit rules of the game that enabled the work of government to be conducted in a way that ensured stability over time while accommodating the inevitable conflicts that arose. Later research by Hennessy (1989 and 1995) has described in detail the inner workings of the Whitehall village and the hidden wiring that connects the institutions of government.

In highlighting the influence of civil servants, Heclo and Wildavsky's analysis found echoes in accounts by former ministers of their time in office, of which there were a number relevant to health policy (for example, Crossman, 1977; Castle, 1980; Fowler, 1991; and Owen, 1992). These accounts challenged the view that civil servants give advice and ministers decide by showing how civil servants themselves were often a source of policy ideas. Some writers went further to argue that relationships between officials and pressure groups in policy communities served to frustrate politicians and to block the implementation of policies that challenged the status quo. Again, however, the static implications of these interpretations were brought into question in the 1980s when the Thatcher Government not only turned its back on the corporatist style of policy-making that had dominated the post-war period, but also initiated reforms to the civil service involving a reduction in the number of civil servants and the creation of executive agencies at arm's length from government. These developments served as a salutary reminder of the continuing influence of political leaders and the vulnerability to change of relationships between civil servants and pressure groups in policy communities.

The 'rediscovery' of the importance of government institutions in policy-making gave rise to a body of research into the workings of the core executive within government (for example Rhodes, 1995), which described the relationship between the Prime Minister, the Cabinet and government departments. The importance of this work was in seeking to shed light on areas of the policy process that had often appeared impenetrable to researchers. As a recent review and synthesis of the evidence has shown, there are no simple ways of characterising the organisation of the core executive and the distribution of power between institutions (Smith, 1999). On the basis of his work, Smith argues that policy is forged out of the interaction between government institutions, which are themselves constrained by the structures and context within which they operate. According to this view, power is everywhere, with influence being determined by the resources at the disposal of different players and the interdependency of these players. This interdependency extends to pressure groups, particularly in policy communities, where the support and co-operation of groups are needed in the implementation of policy.

The other stream of literature relevant to the data we have gathered is that relating to agenda setting. Of particular note in this context is Kingdon's work, which offers a framework for studying the way that conditions come to be defined as problems and are linked to policy solutions through the political process (Kingdon, 1995). Drawing on examples from the USA, Kingdon stresses the complexity of the forces at work. He maintains that visible participants like politicians are important in setting the agenda and hidden participants like civil servants are influential in defining the alternatives for consideration. Within this framework of analysis there are both regular patterns and random occurrences, and no single theory can offer an adequate account of the complexities involved.

As this brief review suggests, a number of concepts are relevant in analysing the evidence reported here. The data we have gathered sheds light on the role of policy networks, and the influence of politicians and civil servants. In exploring these issues, it is important to locate meso-level analysis of the policy process in context and to identify changes in the macro environment that have an impact on what happens within policy networks. Equally, it is necessary to take a dynamic perspective, recognising that relationships change over time and may be influenced by the individuals involved as well as the structures of policy-making. One particular issue to explore is the relationship between networks and outcomes, specifically whether policy communities lead to the pattern of incremental change posited in the literature.

Policy communities

The influence of the BMA as a pressure group and the closeness of its relationship with the Department of Health was attested to by all of the politicians interviewed. This was most apparent in the account given by Kenneth Clarke, who referred not only to the BMA as 'the most unscrupulous trade union I have ever dealt with' but also to the ethos of the Department as being to 'not upset the BMA, not upset the royal colleges, not upset the RCN'. As he also commented, 'The tradition of the Department was based on allowing all these interest groups just to run the whole damn thing'.

These characteristics exemplify behaviour in policy communities and reflect a concern to develop and maintain relationships between organisations expected to do business over time. They are reinforced by the presence on the staff of the Department of a large number of doctors whose loyalties lie as much with their profession as the civil service. Since the establishment of the NHS, the 'mutual dependency' (Klein, 1990, p.700) of the medical profession and the government has played a major part in the shaping of health policy, and the interests of each have been served in the process. As a comparative study of policy networks in the UK and the USA has shown, health policy in Britain involves a relatively stable and cohesive policy community and in this respect is different from health policy-making in the USA and from most other policy areas studied (Smith, 1993).

In view of this, the puzzle that is posed by the data presented here is why did relationships between the Department and the BMA deteriorate during Clarke's tenure as Secretary of State? If a major part of the explanation for this was the style adopted by Clarke and the deliberately belligerent stance he took, other factors were also important. Not least the approach to policy development preferred by Margaret Thatcher during the Ministerial Review of the NHS was exclusive rather than inclusive, centring as it did on a small committee chaired by the Prime Minister herself and not following the processes of consultation and debate usually found in policy communities. This is confirmed by the BMA Chairman at the time, who has noted that as far as the Prime Minister was concerned:

> the BMA leaders were simply turbulent priests whom she would like to be rid of. Throughout her time as Prime Minister, she consistently refused to meet any of them.

(Lee-Potter, 1997, p.91)

Put another way, the rules of the game were suspended in the health policy community because of the antagonistic attitude of the Thatcher Government to the medical profession and its representative bodies, and the Government's preference for policy reviews carried out by small groups to tight deadlines with the minimum of consultation. In a different context, this is how the Griffiths inquiries into general management and community care were conducted. The outcome in both cases was not so much an exhaustive analysis of the issues and options as a succinct report setting out proposals for action. Such an approach was in keeping with the conviction school of politics to which Margaret Thatcher belonged and, while it had the virtue of leading directly to reform in the chosen area, it had the consequence of excluding and provoking groups whose support was often important in securing the implementation of reform.

The conduct of the Ministerial Review therefore illustrates that relationships within the policy community change when powerful actors in government choose to override established routines. As Smith notes, the consequence may be that government incurs costs:

> *Mrs Thatcher was prepared to use her political authority … and capital to challenge an established policy community by making policy outside of it. She realised that if reform was left to the community it would be emasculated and therefore she demonstrated that political actors could take decisions without the support of key interest groups. Nevertheless, this did have costs … the bypassing of the policy community created a high level of ill-feeling amongst doctors and so made the development of policy and, in particular, its implementation more difficult.*

(1993, p.184)

Perhaps for this reason, but also because of the prospect of a general election, the replacement of Kenneth Clarke with William Waldegrave led the Government to seek a rapprochement with the BMA. Margaret Thatcher's brief to Waldegrave was to 'calm them down' and the BMA leaders at the time immediately noticed a change of approach:

> *One feature of Waldegrave's approach, even in formal meetings with others present, was a willingness to explore matters in a non-ideological way quite unlike any of the other ministers with whom I have exchanged views.*

(Lee-Potter, 1997)

The political style of the Thatcher administration had a direct impact on the work of the health secretaries.

This applied not just to the difference of style of the new Secretary of State but also in time to the BMA gaining to access to John Major, who replaced Margaret Thatcher as Prime Minister in 1990. The rebuilding of relationships between the Government and the medical profession continued under Virginia Bottomley and Stephen Dorrell, the approach taken by the latter during the listening exercise on primary care in 1996, in which the BMA was closely involved, clearly indicating a return to more normal relations in the policy community. What this suggests is that while Wistow (1992) was correct at the time of writing in detecting an important shift in the nature of the relationship between the Department of Health and the medical profession within the health policy community, taking a longer-term view the years 1988–90 appear as a temporary aberration in a much longer period of settled and established behaviour.

How then can this shift and the consequent resumption of business as usual be explained? The literature we have reviewed suggests that explanations have to be sought in the macro environment rather than in policy networks themselves. In this period, changes in the economy, which were instrumental in bringing the Thatcher Government to power, were certainly important in stimulating a more radical examination of policy options than had been contemplated previously. The policies pursued by the Government, including privatisation of nationalised industries, controls over public spending, and measures to improve the performance of public services, created conflict with a variety of pressure groups but this was seen by politicians as a price worth paying in order to tackle underlying weaknesses in Britain's economic position. The Government's preferences for markets over bureaucracies was tempered in the case of public services by concerns about the electoral consequences of pursuing outright privatisation, hence the adoption of policies like the NHS internal market, which sought to introduce competitive principles into a publicly financed and largely publicly owned service. Yet in relation to both economic policy and social policy, the political response to changes in the economic environment unsettled corporatist relationships and created a degree of conflict unprecedented in the post-war period.

In reflecting on these developments, it is difficult to escape the conclusion that the policies that were adopted in relation to the NHS would have been impossible to pursue if they had been negotiated through the normal channels in the health policy community. As the subsequent campaign of the BMA in opposition to the internal market showed, the medical profession feared that the Government was intent on privatising the NHS despite protestations to the contrary, and it waged all out war in trying to stop the changes going ahead. Anticipating this, it was little surprise that the Government chose to undertake its review of the NHS without widespread debate and consultation. The reason why conflict between the Government and the BMA did not persist was that implementing the reforms called for the acquiescence if not the active support of the medical profession, thereby lending credence to the argument of writers like Cawson (1982) and Smith (1993), who contend that producer groups like the BMA are in an influential position because of their pivotal role in policy implementation.

While the support of doctors was secured in part by the use of incentives that made it attractive for the medical profession to give its backing to NHS trusts and GP fundholding, other action was also needed. It is this that helps to explain why the Government moved to repair relations with the BMA shortly before the set date for implementation, and also why the presentation of the reforms was softened to make them appear more acceptable. The dependence of government on the medical profession in the implementation of policy meant that even the truncated radicalism of the internal market, constrained as it was by the Government's assessment of what could be sold to the public, was modified further in practice. The role of doctors in implementation therefore meant that the BMA retained considerable power, notwithstanding the willingness of the Thatcher Government to 'take on' what it perceived as entrenched interests. To be sure, the policies pursued did affect the balance of power within the NHS and represented a further stage in the strengthening of the role of 'corporate rationalisers' (to borrow the language of Alford, 1975) and the constraining of medical dominance. Nevertheless, they did not produce the *transformation* sought by politicians. As Marsh and Rhodes (1992a) have observed in their analysis of Thatcherite policies, 'it is the continued existence and power of policy networks which has acted as the greatest constraint on the development and implementation of radical policy' (Marsh and Rhodes, 1992a, p.185).

Politicians, civil servants and policy entrepreneurs

In emphasising the continuing importance of the health policy community in shaping policy outcomes, and the influence of changes in the macro environment on relationships within the policy community, the role of key individuals in government should not be ignored. While this was partly a question of style, it also involved issues of substance.

As we have seen, Margaret Thatcher was insistent that tax relief should be introduced to encourage private medical insurance. Although her main preference was not accepted, she did succeed in getting tax relief accepted for elderly people. Similarly, Kenneth Clarke was influential in promoting the idea of GP fundholding and in pulling together what had been achieved in the Ministerial Review at the time of his appointment into a workable plan for the future. Key individuals continued to be important as the 1990s progressed. William Waldegrave and Virginia Bottomley actively promoted *The Health of the Nation* strategy, and Stephen Dorrell took a close interest in primary care. In all cases, the detail of policy was fashioned with relevant parts of the policy community, but ministers were instrumental in identifying issues for attention and ensuring that they were followed through. This is consistent with Kingdon's argument that politicians have a particular part to play in setting the policy agenda (Kingdon, 1995).

In none of these cases did ministers act alone. The involvement of the Prime Minister and Cabinet in policy-making occurred relatively rarely once the direction of change set out in *Working for Patients* had been agreed, but nevertheless could be important. An example was the debate that occurred over *The Health of the Nation*, a policy that affected several departments and that was only adopted after lively discussions in the core executive during which John Major gave his backing to Virginia Bottomley. Similarly, the involvement of the Chancellor of the Exchequer in health policy was intermittent and when it occurred tended to focus on issues with expenditure implications rather than routine matters of health policy. The experience of Treasury ministers in the Department of Health was a two-edged sword in this context as they knew 'where the bodies were buried', to use Stephen Dorrell's words, and also understood the requirement in political terms for the NHS to be adequately funded.

Equally important were the civil servants in the Department of Health who supported ministers. Although Kenneth Clarke reported that in the early stages of his tenure he had difficulty in obtaining the advice and support he requested, the overwhelming thrust of the evidence reported here is of the reliance of politicians on their officials and a strong sense of partnership in their working arrangements. Time and again, examples were cited of civil servants who played an important part at crucial junctures in the development of policy, with only one notable example of them failing to do their duty. Given that this example involved a presentation to the Prime Minister about the state of readiness to implement the NHS reforms, a degree of nervousness

Richmond House, location of the offices of the secretary of state for health.

and inexperience might be excused. The influence of civil servants extended from policy-making into implementation, most particularly at the point when *Working for Patients* was completed and the NHS Management Executive (as it then was) took responsibility for overseeing the effective delivery of the Government's reforms.

To make this point is not to argue that civil servants presented a united front to ministers. As we have seen, on a number of occasions politicians reported that there were differences of view among officials and they used these differences to clarify their own thinking. An example concerned how many NHS trusts to establish in 1991, with William Waldegrave contrasting the more gung-ho attitude of Duncan Nichol and the caution of Sheila Masters. Yet if debate between civil servants could be useful to ministers, it also carried risks. For this reason, Virginia Bottomley insisted on having meetings with all her senior officials on a regular basis to discuss options and agree on a way forward.

It was during this period that the distinction within the Department of Health between mandarins and managers became particularly apparent (Day and Klein, 1997), illustrating another fault line in the sources of advice available. The NHS Management Executive led the implementation of policy within the Department, and its physical separation in Leeds, insisted on by Kenneth Clarke, signified its distinctive responsibilities. The permanent secretary led the work of the wider Department of Health in London, acting as the 'Whitehall warrior', in Virginia Bottomley's words, to sort out issues within government. While there was no evidence of fundamental conflict between the mandarins and managers from the accounts presented here, these differences indicate that the Department was by no means a monolith. Kenneth Clarke's perception that there was a Departmental view and style may have been accurate at the beginning of this period but as time went on the existence of competing centres of power and influence within the Department resulted in a more pluralistic approach.

As well as relying on civil servants, ministers were heavily dependent on advice and support from the NHS, particularly during the implementation of policy. Given the size of the NHS and the span of control, for the most part ministers worked through regional chairmen who served as their loyal lieutenants in implementing the changes smoothly and on time. As Kenneth Clarke noted, he and Norman Fowler referred to regional chairmen as their 'health cabinet', so close was the working relationship. In some cases, ministers went further and sought direct contact with the chairmen of health authorities and trusts. This was very much Virginia Bottomley's style. Other ministers underlined the importance they attached to the NHS, if not going to the same lengths as Virginia Bottomley, then at least taking time to listen to the opinions of staff and testing out their perceptions against the views of key implementers.

In noting the role of insiders in policy-making, it is worth recalling that the Ministerial Review illustrated the opportunity for participants from outside the policy community to exert influence. This was most apparent in relation to the part played by Alain Enthoven, if not in person then in the power of the ideas he articulated in his written commentaries on the NHS in the 1980s. The influence of Enthoven lends support to Kingdon's analysis of agenda setting and his argument that policy entrepreneurs take advantage of policy windows to link issues that are perceived as problems with potential solutions. In the case of the NHS, think tanks acted as midwives in ensuring the delivery of Enthoven's ideas to the right place, and it was only after this had happened that Enthoven himself re-entered the debate. As Kingdon observes, the role of policy entrepreneurs:

> ... makes sense of the dispute over personality versus structure. When trying to understand change, social scientists are inclined to look at structural changes while journalists emphasise the right person in the right place at the right time. Actually, both are right. The window opens because of some factor beyond the realm of the individual entrepreneur, but the individual takes advantage of the opportunity.

(Kingdon, 1995, p.182)

Enthoven's input to the Ministerial Review is also an example of the phenomenon of policy transfer, an issue that of late has received increasing attention from political scientists (Dolowitz and Marsh, 1996). In this case, transfer was less the result of conscious planning than the availability of an idea that had been developed three years before the Ministerial Review was initiated. At a time when those conducting the Review were casting round for ways of fulfilling the expectations created by the Prime Minister at the outset of the process, and had discarded radical changes to the funding of the NHS, the idea of the internal market served a vital purpose. The policies transferred during the Review were a version of the managed competition model advocated by Enthoven in the USA as well as in other European countries. The irony was that the idea found greater support in Europe than in the USA, even though the conditions for its application were in many respects less favourable.

The way in which the internal market was latched on to during the Ministerial Review is a useful warning to students of the policy process who impute planning and foresight to policy-makers. The adoption of Enthoven's ideas by the Thatcher Government was far more the result of accident than design, representing a way forward after other more radical ideas had been rejected. To be sure, the philosophy of the internal market was consistent with the Government's approach to public policy and can be seen as confirmation of the commitment to fundamentally reform public services. Yet the recollections of those who were closely involved in the production of *Working for Patients* indicate that the idea of the internal market emerged quite late in the review process and found favour only after other alternatives had been discounted.

In offering a solution to one problem, the internal market gave rise to others. Most obviously, the use of this term antagonised those groups whose support was needed to make change work. As we have noted, politicians learned this lesson quickly and altered the presentation of the reforms by using language deemed to be more acceptable. In William Waldegrave's words, 'we had got into a muddle between what was a metaphor and what was reality', and the terms 'market' and 'competition' were replaced by talk of the 'purchaser/ provider system' and, ultimately under Stephen Dorrell, of the 'management reforms'. Despite the shift in terminology, it proved more difficult to persuade managers and clinicians that the market was dead because in many parts of the NHS the metaphor had become the reality. Health policy between 1988 and 1997 therefore illustrates the power of language in politics (Edelman, 1971 and 1977). In the case of the internal market, the Government's initial approach demonstrated how words might make the achievement of policy objectives more difficult by generating opposition from key interests. To move the story on beyond the period covered here, this lesson was not lost on the Blair Government elected in 1997, whose preoccupation with presentation was alluded to indirectly by Virginia Bottomley in reflecting that her approach to the problems of London may have suffered because 'I didn't have enough spin doctors explaining … my strategy'.

Summary

The strong theme running through our analysis is the interdependency that exists in the policy networks surrounding the Department of Health. This lends support to the argument of analysts who draw attention to the complex patterns of relationships both within the core executive and in the policy communities and issue networks that link government departments and pressure groups. The absence of any one centre of power and the existence of government institutions, agencies of sub-government such as health authorities, and pressure groups in constant negotiation with each other defies explanation from any single perspective (Rhodes, 1997).

The evidence we have reported shows how politicians may be in the lead on policy-making but may find their plans modified, often quite significantly, by the need to work with and through other organisations. The strength of the policy community concept is attested to by the restoration of the BMA to its traditional position of influence following its exclusion from the inner circle between 1988 and 1990. Yet accounts that emphasise the role of doctors in policy-making need to be qualified to allow for the evidence we have gathered highlighting the influence of other actors.

We have seen how the BMA shares power both with the civil servants with whom it is in constant contact and with other groups, among whom senior health service managers and chairmen are of most significance. Other contributors to the process of policy-making include academics, researchers and think tanks. The involvement of these actors is, however, more intermittent than that of the major pressure groups and fits the description of issue networks more than policy communities. Similarly, the evidence reported here attests to the influence of individuals who encounter politicians, not formally to negotiate over policy but to debate ideas and issues on social occasions and in other settings.

The view that policy emerges out of policy communities involving established routines and rules of the game therefore needs to be modified to allow for these more random occurrences. In reality, of course, the conversation over dinner between a secretary of state and his or her neighbour that gives rise to a policy idea is not entirely random, as these individuals come together in a context to which only a small proportion of potential participants are invited. Nevertheless, the ability of relatively chance meetings of this kind to have an influence should not be downplayed, nor should the personal musings of politicians themselves, whether on holiday in Galicia (Clarke), in the course of preparing for a major speech (Bottomley), or on a car journey home at the end of a working week (Dorrell). As our research has shown, the previous experience of politicians and the beliefs they bring with them into office are particularly important in shaping the development of policy.

Drawing these strands together, it can be suggested that it is the influence of individuals working within established structures that shapes health policy. The interdependency of these individuals and their interaction with key organisations leads to bargaining and negotiation out of which policy evolves. Politicians are important in shaping the agenda and in working with civil servants to identify and choose between policy options. Outside organisations and interests are involved in this process to a greater or lesser degree, with some like the BMA particularly well placed to influence direction of policy. Periods of relative stability and continuity are interrupted by periods of innovation and change, most obviously when politicians external to policy communities seek to question the established consensus.

The resilience of policy communities can be explained by the need to secure the co-operation of groups in the implementation of policy. This also accounts for the prevailing pattern of incremental rather than step change. Policy communities may be destabilised by developments in the macro economic environment, which stimulate politicians to contemplate options that lie outside the dominant consensus. However, movement in one direction may be followed by change in the opposite direction as the occupants of high office come and go. It is out of the ebbing and flowing of relationships in policy networks that decisions emerge, to be refined and amended during the process of implementation.

To return to the beginning of this chapter, the conclusion suggested by our analysis is that policy communities are structured in a way that makes non-incremental change difficult to achieve. If this is the case, then under what circumstances might such change occur? Two possibilities can be suggested. First, major events like war and economic crises may force a response from politicians that goes beyond the accepted realms of possibilities. It was of course precisely in these circumstances that the NHS was established, with war creating the conditions in which the Attlee Government was able to introduce a comprehensive programme of social reform.

Second, events that cast doubt on the credibility or legitimacy of insider groups like the BMA and the interests they represent may lead to fundamental reforms. This happened in part in 1998 when a series of cases of failures in clinical performance in the NHS led the Government to formulate plans to strengthen the regulation of the medical profession. These cases weakened the ability of doctors to resist policies that in the past had been ruled off the agenda. In Kingdon's terms it created a policy window for linking policy solutions (for example, the introduction of clinical governance and an NHS inspectorate) to issues that had become defined as problems (Kingdon, 1995). While the process of policy development in relation to this episode has yet to be analysed, the combination of circumstances in 1998 led to an unusual opportunity that politicians were quick to seize.

A final thought

The question that remains is the normative one: how could the policy-making process be improved? In this context, the reflections of Robert Reich, Secretary of Labour in the first Clinton Administration and professor of social and economic policy at Brandeis University, cited at the beginning of this book, offer a reference point for thinking about health policy-making in the UK. The essence of Reich's argument is that neither pure analysis nor public opinion polling can substitute a process in which politicians lead debate and engage citizens in deliberation and discussion. Applying this insight to the evidence summarised here, it can be suggested that what is needed to strengthen health policy-making in Britain is a process in which the circle of participants is widened and public involvement does not simply involve politicians making an assessment of the electoral consequences of their actions and drawing on the results of focus group discussions.

To return to the starting point of our discussion, what this indicates is that the corporatist tendencies of the health policy community need to be leavened with a dose of pluralism involving opportunities not only for patient and consumer groups to be consulted but also for dialogue and deliberation to occur in the identification of options and the selection of alternatives. Put another way, innovations in democratic practice (Stewart, 1995) should be encouraged to enable options to be tested and forged in an open environment. Through a process of democratic deliberation, public understanding of the complexities of health policy may be enhanced and the legitimacy of the institutions of government and the decisions that emanate from them reinforced.

References

Alford R. *Health Care Politics*. Chicago: University of Chicago Press, 1975.

Beer SH. *Modern British Politics*. 2nd ed. London: Faber, 1969.

Bottomley V. *The NHS: continuity and change*. London: Royal Society of Medicine, 1995.

Castle B. *The Castle Diaries 1974–76*. London: Weidenfeld and Nicolson, 1980.

Cawson A. *Corporatism and Welfare*. London: Heinemann, 1982.

Crossman RHS. *The Diaries of a Cabinet Minister: Vol. 3, Secretary of State for Social Services 1968–70*. London: Hamilton and Cape, 1977.

Day P and Klein R. *Steering but not Rowing?* Bristol: The Policy Press, 1997.

Department of Health. *The Health of the Nation – a policy assessed*. London: The Stationery Office, 1998.

Dolowitz D and Marsh D. Who Learns What from Whom: a Review of the Policy Transfer Literature. *Political Studies* 1996; XLIV: 343–57.

Eckstein H. *Pressure Group Politics*. London: Allen and Unwin, 1960.

The Economist. Stephen Dorrell's healing touch. 12 August 1995.

Edelman M. *Politics as Symbolic Action*. New York: Academic Press, 1971.

Edelman M. *Political Language*. New York: Academic Press, 1977.

Enthoven A. *Reflections on the Management of the NHS*. London: Nuffield Provincial Hospitals Trust, 1985.

Financial Times. The politics of NHS reform. 18 June 1990.

Fowler N. *Ministers Decide*. London: Chapmans, 1991.

Ham CJ. *Management and Competition in the NHS*. Abingdon: Radcliffe Medical Press, 1997.

Ham CJ. *Health Policy in Britain*. 4th ed. Basingstoke: Macmillan, 1999.

Haywood S and Hunter D. Consultative Processes in Health Policy in the United Kingdom: a view from the centre. *Public Administration* 1982; 69: 143–62.

Heclo H. Issue Networks and the Executive Establishment. In: King A, editor. *The New American Political System*. Washington: American Enterprise Institute, 1978.

Heclo H and Wildavsky A. *The Private Government of Public Money*. London: Macmillan, 1974.

Hennessy P. *Whitehall*. London: Secker and Warburg, 1989.

Hennessy P. *The Hidden Wiring*. London: Gollancz, 1995.

King's Fund. *London Health Care 2010*. London: King's Fund, 1992.

Kingdon JW. *Agenda, Alternatives and Public Policies*. 2nd ed. New York: HarperCollins, 1995.

Klein R. The State of the Profession: The Politics of the Double Bed. *BMJ* 1990; 301: 700–02.

Lee-Potter J. *A Damn Bad Business*. London: Gollancz, 1997.

Lindblom C. The Science of 'Muddling Through'. *Public Administration Review* 1959; 19.

Marsh D and Rhodes R. *Implementing Thatcherite Policies*. Buckingham: Open University Press, 1992a.

Marsh D and Rhodes R. *Policy Networks in British Government*. Oxford: Clarendon Press, 1992b.

Middlemas K. *Politics in Industrial Society*. London: Andre Deutsch, 1979.

Owen D. *Time to Declare*. London: Michael Joseph, 1992.

Reich RB. *Locked in the Cabinet*. New York: Vantage Books, 1998.

Rhodes R. From Prime Ministerial Power to Core Executive. In: Rhodes R and Dunleary P, editors. *Prime Minister, Cabinet and Core Executive*. London: Macmillan, 1995.

Rhodes R. *Understanding Governance*. Buckingham: Open University Press, 1997.

Secretary of State for Health and others. *Working for Patients*. London: HMSO, 1989.

Secretary of State for Health. *The Health of the Nation*. London: HMSO, 1991.

Secretary of State for Health. *The National Health Service: A Service with Ambitions*. London: HMSO, 1996.

Smith M. *Pressure, Power and Policy*. London: Harvester Wheatsheaf, 1993.

Smith M. *The Core Executive in Britain*. Basingstoke: Macmillan, 1999.

Stewart J. *Innovation in Democratic Practice*. Birmingham: Institute of Local Government Studies, 1995.

Thatcher M. *The Downing Street Years*. London: HarperCollins, 1993.

Wistow G. The Health Service Policy Community: Professionals Pre-Eminent or Under Challenge? In: Marsh and Rhodes, 1992b, *op. cit.*

Cast of characters

Donald Acheson, Chief Medical Officer, 1983–91.

Virginia Bottomley, Health Secretary, 1992–95; Minister for Health, 1989–92.

Kenneth Calman, Chief Medical Officer, 1991–98.

Kenneth Clarke, Health Secretary, 1988–90; Minister for Health, 1982–85.

Stephen Dorrell, Health Secretary, 1995–97; Parliamentary Under Secretary of State for Health, 1990–92.

Alain Enthoven, Marriner S Eccles Professor of Public and Private Management, Stanford University, California, 1973–

Andrew Foster, Deputy Chief Executive of the NHS Management Executive, 1991–92.

Christopher France, Permanent Secretary, 1987–92.

Rennie Fritchie, Chairman of South West Regional Health Authority, 1992–96.

Clive Froggatt, GP, Cheltenham.

Peter Griffiths, Deputy Chief Executive of the NHS Management Executive, 1990–91.

Roy Griffiths, Adviser to the Government on the NHS, Deputy Chairman of the NHS Policy Board, 1989–94.

Christine Hancock, General Secretary, Royal College of Nursing, 1989–

Graham Hart, Permanent Secretary, 1992–97.

Strachan Heppell, Deputy Secretary, 1983–95.

Margaret Jay, Director, National Aids Trust, 1988–92; Vice Chair of Parkside Health Authority, 1986–97.

Alan Langlands, Chief Executive of the NHS Executive, 1994–

Jeremy Lee-Potter, Chairman of BMA Council, 1990–93.

Roy Lilley, Chairman of Homewood NHS Trust, 1991–94.

Gerald Malone, Minister for Health, 1994–97.

Sheila Masters, Director of Finance of the NHS Management Executive, 1988–91.

Brian Mawhinney, Minister for Health, 1992–94.

Robert Maxwell, Chief Executive of the King's Fund, 1980–97.

Alan Maynard, Professor of Economics, University of York, 1983–

John Moore, Secretary of State for Social Services, 1987–88.

Julia Neuberger, Chairman of Camden and Islington Community Health Services NHS Trust, 1993–97.

Duncan Nichol, Chief Executive of the NHS Management Executive, 1989–94.

Michael Peckham, Director of Research and Development, 1991–95.

Claire Rayner, writer and broadcaster.

Clive Smee, Chief Economic Adviser, Department of Health (formerly Department of Health and Social Security), 1984–

John Spiers, Chairman of Brighton Health Authority, 1991–92; and of Brighton Health Care NHS Trust, 1992–94.

William Waldegrave, Health Secretary, 1990–92.

William Wells, Chairman of South Thames Regional Health Authority, 1994–96; and then South Thames Regional Office of the NHS Executive.

Donald Wilson, Chairman of Mersey Regional Health Authority, 1982–94; and of North West Regional Health Authority, 1994–96.

John Yates, Director of IACC, University of Birmingham, 1982–